FENG SHUI
FOR BUSINESS

EVELYN LIP

TIMES BOOKS INTERNATIONAL
Singapore • Kuala Lumpur

Dedicated to Kenny and Jacqueline Lip

Photograph on p. 89 courtesy of *Business Times*
© Illustrations by Evelyn Lip
© 1989 Times Editions Pte Ltd
Reprinted 1990, 1991, 1993, 1994, 1995

Published by Times Books International
an imprint of Times Editions Pte Ltd
Times Centre
1 New Industrial Road
Singapore 1953

Times Subang
Lot 46, Subang Hi-Tech Industrial Park
Batu Tiga
40000 Shah Alam
Selangor Darul Ehsan
Malaysia

Printed in Singapore

ISBN 981 204 138 9

Contents

Preface

Feng shui was first practised in ancient China when the people were mainly agriculturalists. To these people wind and water were very powerful natural forces that could either destroy or nurture their crops. When there was a devastating wind their crops would be destroyed. But with constant rainfall their crops would grow and they would benefit from a good harvest.

Chinese geomancy or *feng shui* is about living in harmony with the natural environment and tapping the goodness of nature to benefit man.

Feng shui for Business is written for the business community. It is a guidebook for those who are building or setting up shops, hotels, shopping or office complexes or factories, to tap the good cosmic energy of the earth. You may use this book with or without consultation with a geomancer. It is also a book for students of architecture, practising architects, interior designers, contractors, even readers interested in *feng shui*.

Written as a practical guide, the book begins with a discussion of *feng shui* and business. Chapter two gives an historical background of urban design and *feng shui* as well as rules of thumb for layout and grouping of commercial buildings. The third chapter gives advice on how to choose a site and orient a building. Chapter four discusses *feng shui* and the design of buildings, including form and proportion, daylighting and ventilation, landscaping, lighting and use of colour. It also gives advice on design of specific spaces, from hotels and industrial buildings right down to the office and shop. There is even a section on furniture dimensions which are favourable geomantically.

Chapter five is a guide to picking names and designing signboards and logos for business establishments while chapter six deals with office warming rituals. The last chapter presents many case studies of *feng shui* including renovations of buildings to improve their *feng shui*.

Complete with tables, sketches and diagrams, this book is an easy-to-follow guide to *feng shui* for business.

Acknowledgements

I continue to be indebted to my readers all over the world who have given me much encouragement and demonstrated tremendous interest in my work. Much of the inspiration for this book came from them.

I am also indebted to numerous organisations for inviting me to lecture or talk to them on various topics related to Chinese culture ranging from festivals to Chinese geomancy. Some of them are National University of Singapore; School of Architecture, University of Minnesota, U.S.A.; Environmental Awareness Centre, University of Wisconsin, U.S.A.; School of Architecture, University of Syracuse, New York, U.S.A.; The Urban Development Institute of Australia; The Rotary Clubs of Singapore; the British Association of Singapore; the International Business Women's Association; the Real Estate Developers Associations in Singapore and Malaysia; the Association of Valuers and Property Consultants and the Friends of the National Museum.

Individual readers who have given me much encouragement are too numerous for me to list. But I wish to thank Mr Patrick Horsbrugh (Chairman of the Environic Foundation International, U.S.A.), G. L. Lee (Cambridge, England), Hugh Capstick (England) and Wendy Dubow (Women's World Banking, U.S.A.) for their encouragement.

I thank those who gave me permission to publish case studies and resource materials. Special thanks go to the management of Pinetree town and country club.

My thanks also go to Kenny, my son, and Jacqueline, my daughter who spent many hours typing the manuscript. Last but not least, thanks to members of my immediate family for their ceaseless encouragement and spiritual support during the course of writing this book.

A compass or luopan *is used for geomantic assessment.*

1   *Feng Shui* and Business

Introduction

Feng shui (风水), a term literally translated as wind-water, is the Chinese art of geomancy, the placement and location of buildings and manmade structures to harmonise with, as well as benefit from, the surrounding physical environment. For centuries, *feng shui* has been widely practised among the Chinese, to reassure and benefit the living, although it was originally used to locate propitious sites for the burial of the dead.

This art of divination is called *Kanyu* 堪與 in classical Chinese and *feng shui* 风水 in colloquial Chinese. It is believed that with proper orientation of one's house or business premises one is able to harmonise with nature and relate to the physical surroundings favourably to attract desirable cosmological influences. This belief is not confined to the Chinese alone. In the West, it is known as geomancy (from the Latin word, Geomantia).[1] It was first used by Hugo Sanctallensis in Aragon for Islamic divination.[2] Geomancy is even practised in Africa. Records have been made of geomantic practices in Africa where references were made to four elements, air, fire, earth and water, which were linked to the four quarters of the Universe.[3]

In ancient China, nearly all cities and towns were planned in accordance to *feng shui*, or Chinese geomancy precepts. Commercial buildings were constructed according to the rules of *feng shui*.

The belief of *feng shui* has spread far and wide especially in Asia. It was introduced to Japan during the Tang dynasty.[4] The precepts of Japanese geomancy on commercial buildings are similar to those of the Chinese although the Japanese do not apply it to burial places. Also, in Japan, the application of *feng shui* was extended to garden design. The. Japanese believe in the creation of harmony of landscape to enhance a building's setting.

In the Saihoji, one of the oldest gardens in Japan, built in the 13th century, symbolic elements derived from Chinese mythology are used. Rocks representing the Eight Immortals sitting on tortoises depict longevity.

1

In Vietnam, where the Chinese had ruled from the second century B.C., cities were built according to the Chinese geomantic rules.[5]

In Southeast Asia and Hong Kong, many believe that *feng shui* can enhance or destroy one's luck. Having good *feng shui* builds up one's confidence and energy to pursue success. It is believed that having bad *feng shui* may lead one to misfortune, failure in business ventures, or poor health.

When the 47-storey Hongkong and Shanghai Bank in Hong Kong was completed and banking business about to begin, a geomancer was engaged to choose an auspicious date for the opening ceremony. True to the dictates of *feng shui*, the building sits at the foot of Victoria Peak and faces the sea, with the hill on its back to protect it and the view in front to enhance its wealth. Even the building plans were checked by the geomancer. The original structural system of the building was changed to ensure good luck (see sketches below for comparison of the original structural design and final design, as well as the building itself).

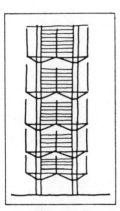

*The original
structural system.*

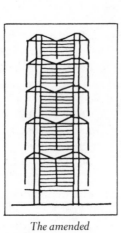

*The amended
structural system.*

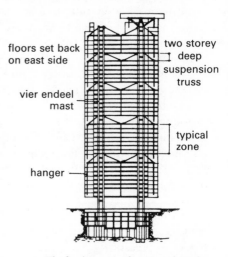

The final structural system adopted.

2

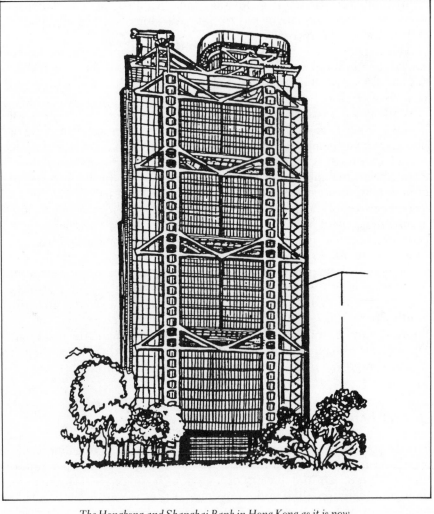

The Hongkong and Shanghai Bank in Hong Kong as it is now.

In another instance of geomantic modification, the circular glass windows of the Connaught Centre, also in Hong Kong, was replaced with reflective glass panels.

A site with good *feng shui* can be ruined by interference from undesirable influences. A spire or a chimney are geomantically less than desirable because they each emanate an imbalanced force which can easily overpower or cause imbalance to the built environment.

While it is not possible to change the lay of the land, for valley cannot be transformed into mountain, and water cannot be turned back, a site or building can be geomantically improved to enhance or alter its *feng shui*.

A case in point is the Singapore Hyatt. Originally, the entrance doors to the foyer and the cashier's desk were parallel to the main road. In geomantic terms, wealth flowed out of the hotel too easily. As the doors faced northwest, undesirable spirits could enter without difficulty and assert a malevolent influence upon the business. When a geomancer was consulted, he had the main doors realigned at an angle to the road to retain wealth and to repel evil influences. The fountains directly in front of the hotel were replaced by flower-beds. Two new fountains were built on either side of the main doors and maintained at a certain height to bring prosperity. A flag pole, also in front of the hotel, was removed to the fourth floor, and a Chinese boat to signify the "safe voyage" of the business venture, was made and placed in the restaurant on the first floor. Prayers were also offered for successful business. It appears that the hotel's business improved greatly following the geomantic adjustments.

Qi and *Feng Shui*

The dragon, supreme animal in Chinese mythology, is metaphorically applied to topography, and it is the task of the geomancer to determine the *qi* (氣) or cosmic breath of the dragon, often best located in undulating land resembling the physique of the dragon, in order to site buildings in such a way as to benefit from its vitalising power. As far back as 3,000 years ago, government residences and imperial palaces in China were built according to *feng shui* precepts, which subsequently influenced the Japanese, who apparently chose the sites of Nara and Kyoto for their good *feng shui* qualities.

The rise and fall of the land represent geomantically the advance or retreat of the dragon. The ground must be hard and solid, with a good profile like that of a dragon, if it is to be a good site. The soil or sand, and the water sources, are factors in geomantic study as well.

With the help of the *luopan* or geomancer's compass, the geomancer determines the best orientation of buildings, and assesses the good and bad qualities of the dragon at the site. The *luopan* is a circular disc marked with concentric circles of Chinese characters. It gives series of directions derived from the ancient *Yi Jing* or *Book of Changes* and classifies a variety of geomantic factors such as the type of water and the five orders of nature (or Five Elements) in relation to the time of birth of the owner or prospective buyer. A complicated *luopan* may have as many as 36 concentric circles intricately calibrated.

Qi need not always be beneficial. Evil influences prevail when *yin* and *yang* elements are in discord, and *sha qi* (杀气) or harmful breath could be the result, unless modifications to the landscape or structures are made to create a balance of beneficial forces. Beneficial *qi* or *qi* that gives life and promotes growth is known as *sheng qi* (生气).

Besides the *luopan*, the geomancer uses the geomancer's ruler to calculate the size and overall dimensions of a building to ensure proportions favourable to good fortune. Certain dimensions are considered auspicious, others are to be avoided. In his study of buildings too, the geomancer pays particular attention to the alignment of doors, the primary means by which cosmic breath enters a building and nourishes it. In matching owner to building the geomancer considers the year and time of birth of the owner, and the orientation of the building.

Apart from the surrounding land and the building itself, each room is seen independently to possess *qi*, and the geomancer's task is to locate its nucleus, the centre of vibrant energy, so that its occupants may benefit from it, through the arrangement of furniture or the organisation of work.

Because the whole cosmos is regarded as organically in a state of flux, the orientation of *qi* is not static: it changes every 20 years, a major change occurring every 60 years. (See pages 14 to 19 for diagrams of *qi* areas until the year 2043.) A commercial building with good *feng shui* does not necessarily remain so permanently; its beneficial ambience may be affected subsequently by new buildings in the vicinity, the changing orientation of *qi*, a change in ownership, extensions made to the existing building or alterations in neighbouring buildings.

Yin/Yang Elements and *Feng Shui*

According to Chinese beliefs *yin* and *yang* are complementary forces that underpin all things in existence. Everything in the universe can be classified as either *yin* or *yang*. Masculinity, brightness, colours that are warm, solidity and protrusion are *yang*. *Yin* refers to the opposite of *yang*, such as, feminity, darkness, colours that are cool, liquidity and intrusion.

In order to achieve good *feng shui*, there must be a good balance of *yin* and *yang*. For example, the interior of an office should not be decorated in completely warm or completely cool colours. If the walls of the office are painted a cool colour, the furnishing should be in warm colours. This will strike a balance of *yin* and *yang* colours and, therefore, equilibrium in the office interior. (See pages 46 and 47 on lighting and colour.)

The Five Elements and *Feng Shui*

The Five Elements were conceived as the five forces of nature by the Chinese as early as the 4th century B.C., and designed in the sequence, gold, wood, water, fire and earth. They may be positioned in order of destruction or harmony. The sequence of harmony is gold, water, wood, fire and earth. The sequence of destruction is gold, wood, earth, water and fire. In naming a business establishment for example, the words must be positioned in the order of harmony. (See chapter on *Feng Shui* Names and Signboards for Commercial Buildings.)

The time of birth of a person indicates his Element of birth. If a person is born at 8 am, his Element of birth is earth (see table on page 38). His Element of birth will determine his favourable orientation. If his Element is earth, then his favourable orientation is east-southeast.

Feng Shui and Commercial Buildings

Why is good *feng shui* of buildings necessary for good business? A building functions in terms of exclusion of weather and efficiency in spatial and structural concept. Besides architectural and structural functions, a commercial building also has a psychological function as people are involved in the total machinery of a business establishment.

There is a right time and a right place to sign a contract or seal a business deal and *feng shui* in business is about placement of buildings and the timing of doing things. A building with good *feng shui* is one that allows successful meeting of the minds of business people. It is a place where ambience and environment provide for harmonious expressions of business collaborators to ensure success in business meetings. A sense of physical well-being and emotional equilibrium can be felt when there is balanced *qi* and *yin/yang* elements in the environment and when *qi* revitalises the built environment.

Placed in a world of slightly chaotic and highly competitive nature, a businessman needs to feel a sense of equilibrium in order to maintain a clear mind and achieve success.

Feng shui can lead to good aesthetic sense in architecture. In its advocacy for balance and harmony, the proper relationships between commercial buildings and land, and by extension, man and nature, it tends to lead away from extremes of architecture towards proportion and moderation. Its sensitivity to its human and physical environment has meant emphasis, architecturally, on the unified whole, with harmony striven for from the contribution of many component parts.

7

Footnotes

1 Geomantia is also referred to as divination associated with geological phenomena. The Arabs called it the "science of sand."

2 Smith, E., and Smith, M., *Islamic Geomancy and 20th Century Divinatory Device*, Undena Publications, California, 1980, p.1.

3 Hebert, J.C., "Analyse Structure des Geomancies comoriens Malgaches et Africaines", 1961, *Journal de la Societe des Africanists*, Vol XXXL.

4 Sansom, G., A *History of Japan*, London, 1958, p. 213.

5 Bezacier, L., "Conception du plan des anciennes citadelles-capitales du Nord Vietnam", *Journal Asiatique* CCXL Fasc2, 1952.

2   Urban Design and Commercial Buildings

Historical Background

The Chinese developed orderly and well planned cities as far back as 2000 B.C. Their chessboard-like grid-patterned cities were so methodical in concept that the rulers were able to exercise disciplined control and allow economic, cultural and social development. These cities were also planned for safety against fire hazards, facilitating water supply and circulation. Walled enclosures provided security to the town settlements. Each housing unit was also based on the walled enclosure concept. Some cities even had three enclosing walls to guard them against invasions from foes and evil spirits.

As far back as 3,000 years ago the Chinese applied the concept of *yin* and *yang* to their city planning.[1] *Yin* was represented by an even number and *yang* an odd number. Thus city boundary walls were built in such a way that the length and breadth were unequal, one of *yin* dimension and the other of *yang* dimension. The city was walled in, with streets running east to west or north to south. The wall was considered *yin* and the streets, *yang*.

On the northern side there should be, ideally, hills at the back as protective elements. There should be flowing streams and low hills to the east as symbols of wealth, ponds or lakes to the south also for wealth, and low hills and roads to the west as protective and functional elements.[2]

The Chinese had long been worshippers of nature and they believed that the world was teeming with living things. Everything on the earth lived — the plants, the rocks, the hills and the mountains. The gods and immortals dwelt in the mountains. Thus the land must be respected and its topography and vegetation considered when a structure or an entire city was to be built on it. Meandering streams and undulating topography were signs of good influences. Sharp bends or straight lines meant poor influences.

The *feng shui* theory of planning, Confucian ideals and ancient Chinese social and political hierarchy were clearly reflected in the plans of ancient cities. For example, cities built before and during the Han dynasty (206 B.C.-220 A.D.) were square in plan, the square symbolising the earth. They were enclosed by city walls, each wall having three gate openings as the number three symbolises growth. There were nine main roads running east to west and north to south, the number nine symbolising longevity. To the east, temples for ancestor worship were built, and to the west were the temples for the local deities. The emperor's palace was on the north-south axis and on the highest ground. Changan, the capital city, was built in such a manner. (See sketch below.)

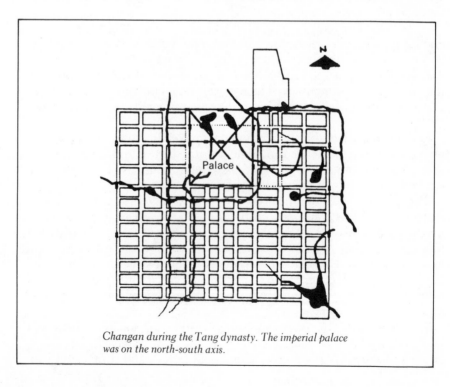

Changan during the Tang dynasty. The imperial palace was on the north-south axis.

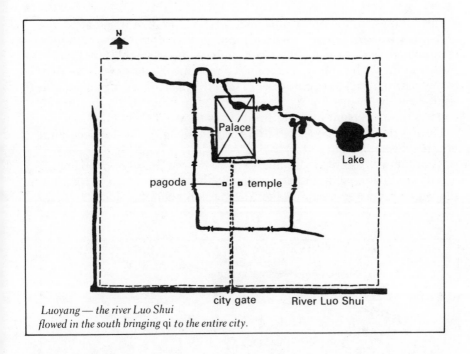

Luoyang — *the river Luo Shui*
flowed in the south bringing qi *to the entire city.*

Another city, Luoyang, built during the Wei period (220-265 A.D.), was also built on a site with good *feng shui*. It had the Yi Mang mountain to its north and the river Luoshui to its south. The palace was in the northern part but on the main axial line of the city. The entire city was enclosed by a wall while the imperial city was encircled by an inner wall and moat. The entrance of the imperial city was designed according to *feng shui* principles. A manmade stream flowed past the three succeeding gates to symbolise wealth and success for the royal family. Along the central axial line, immediately after the second entrance gate on the left and right, were the temples of ancestral worship and a nine-tier *feng shui* pagoda.

The Chinese were not the only people who built their urban areas in a rectilinear pattern. Their western counterparts too built their cities and commercial centres in a chessboard pattern. For example, in France, Rouen in the 10th century was built in a rectilinear pattern with the river Seine passing its main entrance. The city plan was ordered and in equilibrium with roads at right angles to one another. Even the French concept of urban planning then coincided with the dictates of geomancy.

During the Jin period (265-420 A.D.) Jian Kang city was indeed built on a good *feng shui* site. At its back was the hill, Ji Long Shan, on its east was another hill, Zong Shan, and to its south was the river Qin Huai. It was on undulating ground that resembled the twist and turn of a dragon site with revitalising breath of life. (See sketch below.)

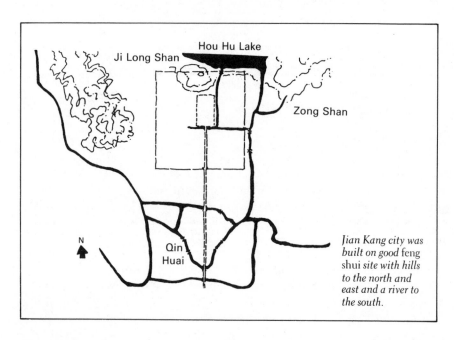

Jian Kang city was built on good feng shui *site with hills to the north and east and a river to the south.*

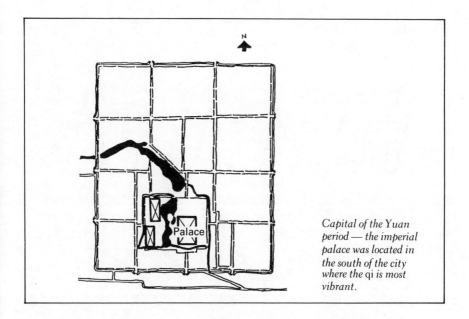

Capital of the Yuan period — the imperial palace was located in the south of the city where the qi is most vibrant.

It is interesting to note that by the Yuan dynasty (1206-1368 A.D.), the plan of the city had changed slightly in that the imperial palace was not built in the northern part of the walled city. Instead it was built in the south along the axial line. (See sketch above.) Why was it so. This is because the location of *qi* in the earth changes every 20 years (see pages 14 to 19 for *qi* areas until the year 2043). During the Wei and Jin periods the *qi* in the square city was most vibrant in the north along the central axial line for a city facing south. But during the Yuan period the main *qi* area was concentrated in the south central region. Thus the Yuan rulers were wise to build the imperial palace in the south instead of the north. In assessing the ancient cities it can be concluded that the imperial palaces were built on the main *qi* locations and imperial sites moved according to the change of *feng shui*.

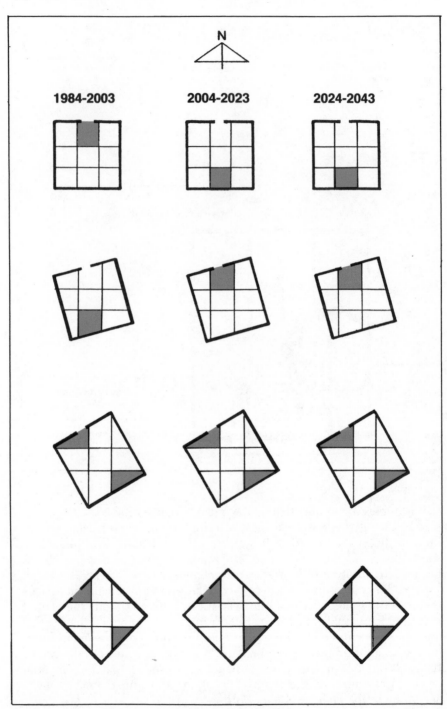

Qi locations until 2043

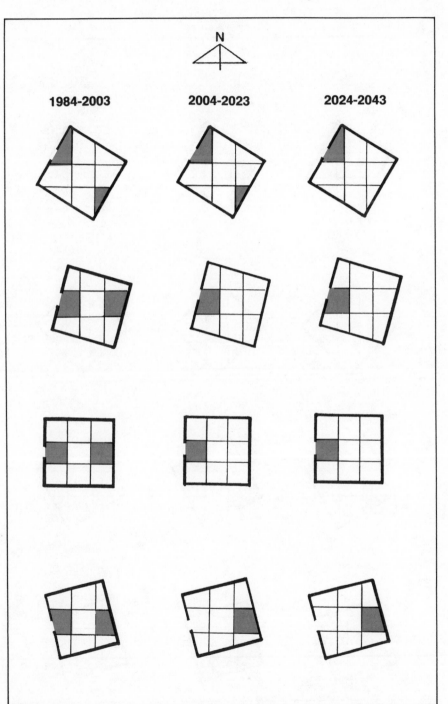

N

1984-2003   **2004-2023**   **2024-2043**

Qi locations until 2043

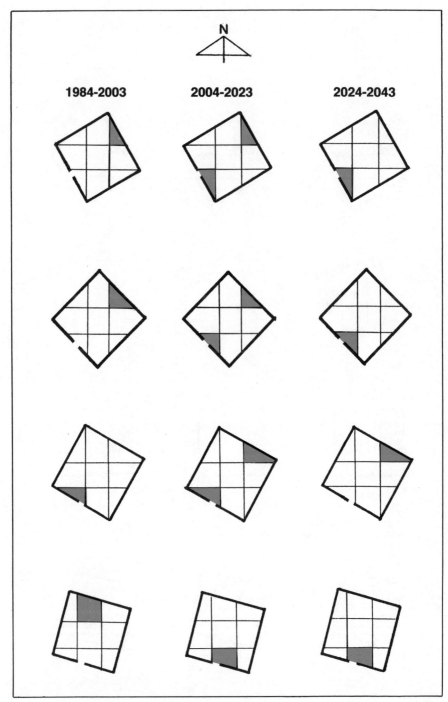

Qi locations until 2043

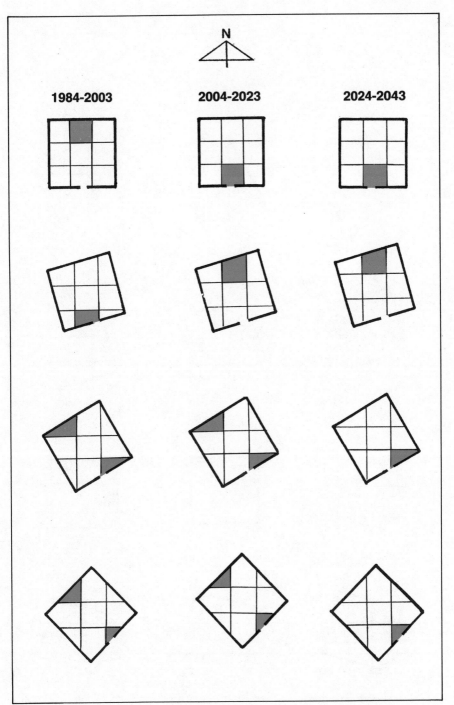

Qi locations until 2043

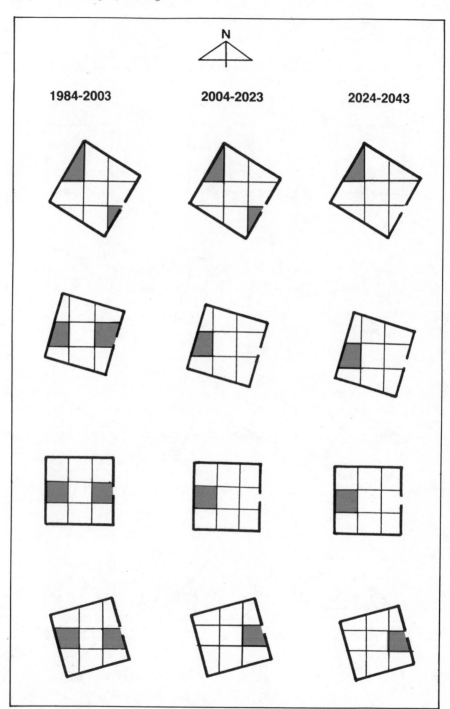

Qi locations until 2043

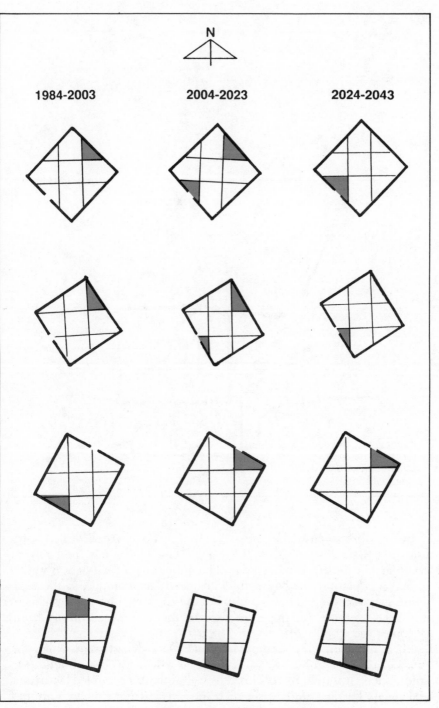

Qi locations until 2043

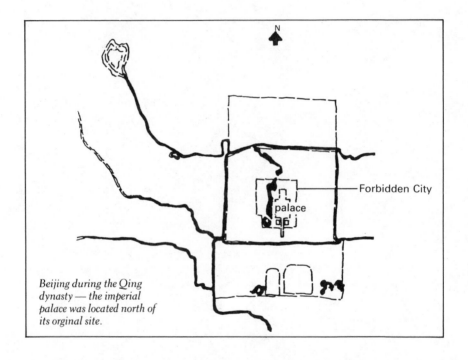

Beijing during the Qing dynasty — the imperial palace was located north of its orginal site.

By the Ming dynasty the imperial palace complex was relocated north from its original site within the capital city of Beijing, probably in accordance with the *qi* movement. The entire city of Beijing was walled in and was planned in symmetry with the palace complex as the focal point. Entrances to the lower portion of the city were through seven gates and accesses into the upper portion of the city were through nine imposing gates.

The Forbidden City of the Ming and Qing dynasties in which the imperial palace complex was situated, and which was out of bounds to commoners, was not only enclosed by walls but also encircled by streams and moats for *feng shui* reason. To the left and right of the City just outside the imperial complex were temples and ceremonial altars for ancestor worship. The dimensions of the Forbidden City (960m×760m) must have met with geomantic requirement. Entrances were provided at the east, south, west and north.

Within the Forbidden City there were many *feng shui* features. For example, the main entrance, Wu Men, led to the Golden Water Bridge beneath which was the Golden Water River, a symbol of glory, magnificence and wealth. The Golden Water Bridge was made up of five bridges, the number five coinciding with the Five Elements. The bridge harmonised with the Golden Water River as it resembled the dragon which was a *yang* symbol while the water in the river was a *yin* symbol.

Golden Water Bridge

Hierarchy of height, form, space and structure was demonstrated by the way the entire complex was built. The three main palaces, Tai He Dian, Zhong He Dian and Bao He Dian, were raised on tiers of marble platforms for *feng shui* reasons as well as for marking the importance of the palaces. Bronze sculptures of the tortoise and crane, both symbolising longevity, and other *feng shui* elements were displayed in the open courts. The colour scheme of the palaces was based on *feng shui* and even the furniture such as chairs were made according to dictates of *feng shui* with the back rest higher than the two arm rests.

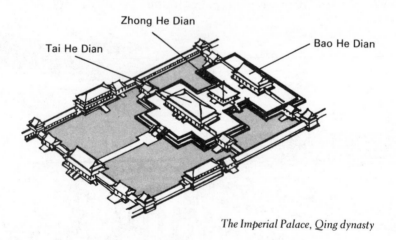

Zhong He Dian

Tai He Dian

Bao He Dian

The Imperial Palace, Qing dynasty

Events in Chinese history also concur with *qi* movement according to the 20-year *feng shui* cycle as described in the *Le Shu Tu*.

In 714 A.D. the *qi* according to the *Le Shu Tu* was believed to be in the south of China. But the capital cities of Luoyang and Changan were not in the south. *Feng shui* was not ideal and by 881 A.D. rebels created a great deal of problem for Emperor Si Zong.

In 891 A.D. when the *sheng qi* of the earth was centred in the south of

China, rebels captured the northern territories. Internal troubles persisted until 904 A.D. and by then the Emperor was murdered. This proved that it did not augur well for the Emperor when *qi* was exhausted at the capital city of his kingdom.

In 1261 A.D., when Kublai Khan assumed power in China, he was wise to establish his capital in the north. He moved the seat of government to Beijing most probably because he was informed that *qi* was concentrated in the northern region.

Grouping of Commercial Buildings

In locating commercial and business centres it is important to find the dragon and *qi* areas. Locate the most important buildings in the *qi* and prominent positions. Bring life into the commercial centres by introducing open and semi-open landscaped courtyards so that there is a contrast of *yin* and *yang* — open and built up areas respectively. Provide amenities such as covered walkways, linked passages and overhead bridges for easy and safe circulation. If possible create vistas to highlight certain important commercial buildings. Create green areas and "lungs" within a highrise and densely built commercial area. Ensure the commercial buildings are grouped in such a way that there is balance in terms of building height and architectural treatment and harmony in terms of economic activities. The most important buildings are to be located in the central position and on the highest ground.

If there are hills and sea in the location, place the commercial buildings facing the sea with the hills in the rear. If there are streams or rivers, make use of these natural water courses to enhance the manmade buildings by integrating them into the scheme.

Feng shui concerns the intangible aspects of the built environment. It also concerns the shape, form and planning of a building and how it is related to the surrounding buildings. The following rules of thumb apply in the grouping and layout of commercial buildings:

A group of buildings with hills at the back.

- It is undesirable to build a row of commercial buildings in various heights, shapes, forms and sizes completely unrelated because this means imbalance in *feng shui*. (See sketch below.)

It is undesirable to build a row of buildings in unrelated heights.

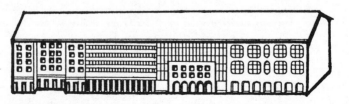

Terraced buildings which are balanced and unified in height.

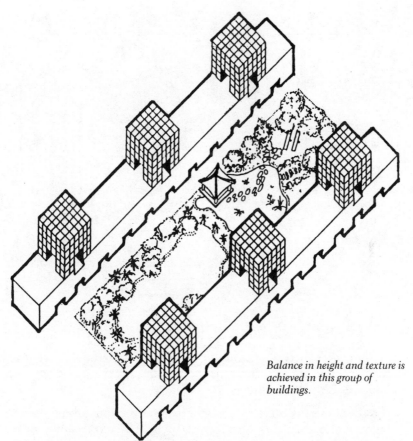

*Balance in height and texture is
achieved in this group of
buildings.*

- It is good *feng shui* practice to design a row of commercial buildings
with unifying architectural or constructional features. For example,
if one of the buildings is of load-bearing bricks, those that are built
after it and next to it should be also of load-bearing bricks or be
related to or similar to load-bearing brick construction. This
enhances the unity and compatibility of the *feng shui* of the
buildings. (See sketch above.)

  A good example is the Plaza of the Rockefeller Centre at New
York which is framed by other buildings. These six storeyed
identical blocks along the Fifth Avenue are of similar architectural
style and treatment, construction materials and finishes to provide
harmony, unity and balance. In short, good *feng shui*.

- It is desirable to introduce unifying features to several blocks of
commercial buildings in one area of a town by introducing
common heights in podiums, colonnades and roofs to achieve
balance. To cite a good example, the Lincoln Centre in New York

25

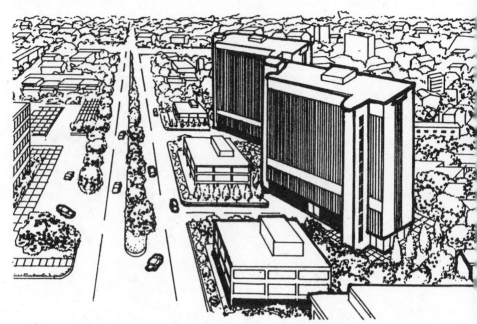

Commercial complex sited at an angle to the T-junction to avoid sha qi.

is planned in an axial organisation with similar rhythm for structural bays and a unifying height for the podium on the first floor. (See photo of Lincoln Centre on page 49.)

- If a shophouse is built in a row of shophouses that are five storeys high, it also should be five storeys high. If it is one storey or ten storeys, there will be imbalance and the shopkeepers will not prosper. On the other hand if the shophouse is very narrow in width while its neighbouring shops are very wide in frontage it is also bad *feng shui*.

- It is not appropriate to clad offices in very reflective glass curtain walls because they are sources of glare to others. In *feng shui*, the glare is a source of *sha qi*. In hot tropical countries such glass walls retain heat and cause heavy loading on the airconditioning plants. In *feng shui*, this retained excessive heat causes imbalance to the *yin/yang* of the *qi*.

- In the layout of commercial buildings it is important to avoid T-junctions that confront the front door or main office spaces or prime shopping areas. T-junctions allow *qi* that is too vibrant to penetrate the building, causing undesirable influence on the building. If a T-junction situation arises, locate the builing to avoid *sha qi* as shown in the drawing above.

- Dimensional coordination should be applied to a group of commercial buildings constructed in a row and on opposite sides of the road. It is undesirable to have a range of unrelated dimensions of window sizes or structural bays.

- Even colour scheme plays a part in the design of a group or row of commercial buildings. Again, harmony and balance is essential to create a good *feng shui* environment. For example, if a shop is painted brown it will appear awkward and inappropriate when the rest in the row of shops are painted white. If the roof tiles of a terrace shophouse is green it will look like an alien if its neighbouring linked shophouses have red roof tiles. Therefore, balance and harmony should be the aim at all levels of design. If contrast is to be introduced to one shophouse the rest should also have some contrast within their facade treatment.

- Plazas and landscaped open and semi-open courtyards are necessary amenities to a large built-up commercial area to give spatial relief, focal points and to act as the *yin* element contrasting with the *yang* or the built-up area.
  If the building is very tall (say 80 metres in height), though it is set back about 30 metres from the street in a plaza, it would still take people by surprise. If the plaza is not enclosed by walls or buildings, it is not very well defined and it does not retain the *qi* as well as if it has boundary walls.

- The road is not just a means of getting from one place to another. It is a conductor of *qi*. It should be so designed that it does not conduct *sha qi* to a commercial building. When a road is winding or meandering it is less likely to upset a state of equilibrium. However, a straight road is still most efficient and gives a good sense of direction.

In America, examples of successful planning of the city and commercial centres are numerous. For example, the Rockefeller Centre has excellent pedestrian spaces and generous circulation corridors which serve the buildings and bring much life and activity. The seasonal plants in the central open space soften the built forms bringing the entire environment closer to nature.

A good designer looks at the terrain in the layout of buildings. Prominent landscape features such as hills, valleys, ponds must be noted and considered for integration into the overall layout. Routes of movement affect the flow of qi. These passageways and routes must be planned in relation to the natural topography and to the commercial buildings.

Footnotes

1 See Nan Hai Guan, *Kanyu Xue Yuan Li* (*The original theory of feng shui*), Hong Kong, 1971, p. 75.
2 See Lip, Evelyn, *Chinese Geomancy*, Times Books International, Singapore, 1979. Also see Skinner, Stephen, *The Living Earth Manual of Feng Shui*, Routledge and Kegan Paul, London, 1982, p.4.

3 *Feng Shui* and the Siting and Orientation of Commercial Buildings

Buildings should be located and built to harmonise with the surrounding buildings and fit into the surrounding built environment and natural elements. For achieving success and prosperity commercial buildings should be oriented according to the horoscope of the owner and with reference to the surrounding environment. However, if the business house has many owners, it should be oriented in accordance with the *Yi Jing*. (See pages 34 to 37.)

Some geomancers orient buildings according to the date of establishment. For example, a commercial establishment which starts operation on the first day of the eighth lunar month in 1988 may be oriented west although people do not favour it as it is the direction of the setting sun. If business starts on the first day of the eighth lunar month in 1989, then the business premises should be oriented south. Some people do not favour the northwest or southwest directions because they are reputed to be unlucky directions or doors of the devils. As can be seen, compatibility of date and direction changes from year to year. Refer to the *Tong Shu*, which is published yearly, for dates and favourable directions.

Most geomancers regard the following factors as most vital to the success of commercial buildings:

- the orientation of the building in relation to the surrounding physical environmental factors

- the orientation of the main door of the building in relation to the owner's horoscope or with reference to the *Yi Jing*

- the *yun* 運 (luck) of the owner or owners and

- the virtue of the owner or owners and the management of the staff in charge of the business.

Picking the Site

When selecting the site for a building it is best to look for a real "dragon" which in a city simply means a main road. The floor area and shape of the site must also be carefully examined. Certain shapes are regarded as good or bad feng shui as shown in the diagrams below.

A site could be in the shape of a square, triangle, rectangle, oval, T, cross, or it could be irregular. A square shaped site is generally regarded as good and is even more suitable for the building of temples and religious establishments because the square shape is classified as a *yin* shape which is spiritual. Rectangular lots are considered good especially when they are longer on the north and south sides.

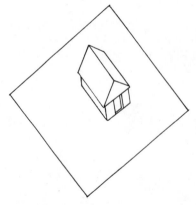

Triangular shapes are unpopular because the net usable spaces are affected by the tips of the triangles. For centuries geomancers have had certain prejudice against triangular lots.

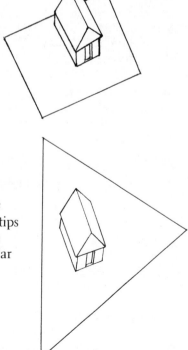

Oval-shaped lots are good for religious buildings because most of their boundary walls are surrounded by other building lots. In *feng shui* such lots are considered neither *yin* nor *yang* lots.

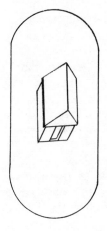
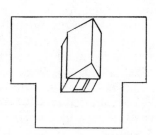

Most T-, cross- and irregular-shaped sites are regarded as unfavourable because it is difficult to build on such awkwardly shaped lots.

Neighbouring lots and buildings, and the type of business to be carried out must also be considered when picking a site for a business. For example, if it is a shop selling food, and your neighbouring shops sell pets or goods that produce unpleasant smells or dust, your business may be affected.

There should be easy access, efficient car parking facilities and public transport to the site. Service areas and roads must be easily accessible.

Visibility of the site should be good. For example, if it is situated on the inner bend of a curved street, it may not be as easily noticed as if it is on a straight street. Although a T-junction provides good visibility, it is to be avoided. (See page 26.)

The land on the right side of the building, known in *feng shui* as the white tiger, should be lower than that on the right, which is known as the azure dragon.

Water flowing past the side of a building does not enhance its *feng shui*. It should pass by its front door. This is why a manmade stream passes the main gate of the Forbidden City in Beijing, China.

A fast-flowing river has more power to erode than a meandering one, hence, a river which flows very fast has *sha qi*, and symbolically erodes wealth. Geomancers believe that it is good to place commercial buildings on the banks of a slow-moving river because the river builds up its bed and bank with alluvium. An explanation could be that very often, the flat plains of such a river contain the best agricultural land. Also, rivers have always been used as a means of transport and irrigation.

It is most vital to locate the source and the mouth of a river, and discharge of water into drains or lakes or water courses. Generally it is a good sign to have the source of water in abundance of supply.

In the 2nd century A.D., Ostia, situated along the Tiber River, was a boom town. The construction of an artificial harbour on the Tyrrhenican Sea increased its importance as the major port of Rome. The harbour generated economic activity because it had good *feng shui* in the first place.

In classical literature there are records of unsuitable site conditions for commercial buildings. Some of the conditions are:

- when the ground is made up of sandy and wet ground

- when grass or plants cannot grow

- when the ground at the back is lower than that in front

- when the south side of the site is high and the north side is low

- when the surrounding ground is high and the actual site is sunken

- when the ground is filled with sand

- when the ground is a deserted piece of land especially after a fire outbreak

- when the site is at the end of a cul-de-sac or T-junction.

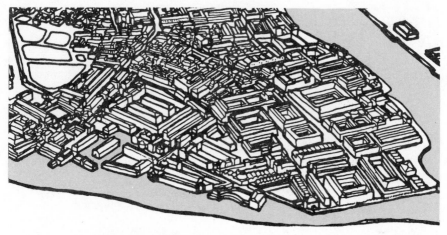

Ostia was a prosperous town because its feng shui *was good.*

Orientation and Other Influences

Many cultures and philosophies draw upon ancient practices, and systems and concepts of thinking. The Chinese believe that the *Book of Changes* or *Yi Jing* contains the unconscious awareness and the mind of man. It is a means whereby man can enquire about his destiny through gaining intuitive knowledge of himself in relation to the rest of the world. The 64 hexagrams in the *Yi Jing* symbolically represent the rhythm of the world. Each hexagram is represented by a six-line diagram which represents attributes, destiny and situations related to man and places. (See diagram on right.)

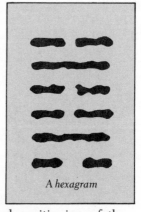

A hexagram

For business establishments the orientation and positioning of the business premises are of vital importance. If the company is a private establishment, the horoscopes of the owner and managing director have to be considered for the location and orientation of the place of operation. (See table for time of birth, Element of birth and favourable orientation on page 38.) If the company is a public organisation, then the hexagrams of the *Yi Jing* should be consulted on the orientation of the business premises (i.e. the direction of the front door). The table below shows the name of the hexagram, the degree of deviance from the North and the symbolic implication of the hexagram in terms of possible success or failure.

Hexagrams	Degree of deviance from North	Symbolic implications
Kun 坤	0°	great capacity and unlimited vigour but could face problems at times
Fu 复	5.625°	uncertainty and free growth
Yi 颐	11.25°	moderate growth and progress
Chun 屯	16.875°	progress and success although setbacks encountered
Yi 益	22.5°	moderate progress
Zhen 震	28.125°	setbacks encountered but, with determination, success achieved
Shi Ke 噬嗑	33.75°	strength balanced by equal weakness
Sui 随	39.375°	firmness and progress
Wu Wang 无妄	45°	motivation and strength moderate progress
Ming Yi 明夷	50.625°	small growth and inactivity
Ben 贲	56.25°	moderate success but setback encountered
Ji Ji 既济	61.875°	limited success and attainment with occasional setback
Jia Ren 家人	67.875°	constancy and success
Feng 丰	73.125°	development and success
Li 离	78.75°	changes and progress
Ge 革	84.375°	advantage and satisfaction; changes made for progress

Hexagrams	Degree of deviance from North	Symbolic implications
Tong Ren 同人	90°	progress and harmony
Lin 临	95.625°	flourish and support
Sun 损	101.25°	restraint and slow progress
Jie 节	106.875°	control and perseverance to gain achievement
Zhong Fu 中孚	112.5°	honesty and sincerity to achieve success
Gui Mei 归妹	118.125°	halt and reconsideration; care should be taken in choice of business
Kui 睽	123.75°	minor success and obstruction
Dui 兑	129.375°	success and progress attained after perseverance
Lu 履	135°	satisfaction, setbacks encountered
Tai 泰	140.625°	good fortune and success
Da Chu 大畜	146.25°	renewal and strength
Xu 需	151.875°	patience and success
Xiao Chu 小畜	157.5°	slow progress and success
Da Zhuang 大壮	163.125°	constancy and strength
Da You 大有	168.75°	vigour and bright future
Kuai 夬	174.375°	renewal and slow growth
Qian 乾	180°	surprising success and firmness

Hexagrams	Degree of deviance from North	Symbolic implications
Hou 姤	185.625°	setbacks encountered
Da Guo 大过	191.25°	flexibility and changes; moderate turnover
Ding 鼎	196.875°	progress and success
Heng 恒	202.5°	success and constancy
Sun 巽	208.125°	average attainment and success
Jing 井	213.75°	stimulation and incompleteness
Gu 蛊	219.375°	destruction and decay
Sheng 升	225°	progress and slow improvement
Song 讼	230.625°	obstruction and apprehension
Kun 困	236.25°	sacrifice and improvement; setbacks encountered
Wei Ji 未济	241.875°	limited success; eventual achievement
Jie 解	247.5°	movement and manifestation
Huan 涣	253.125	dispersion and progress
Kan 坎	258.75°	changes and setbacks encountered
Meng 蒙	264.375°	firmness and confidence but difficulties encountered
Shi 师	270°	commanding and demanding; ups and downs encountered

Hexagrams	Degree of deviance from North	Symbolic implications
Dun 遁	275.625°	slow success and progress
Han 咸	281.25°	influence and success
Lu 旅	286.875°	caution and improvement
Xiao Guo 小过	292.5°	setbacks with moderate success
Jian 渐	298.125°	slow and steady; eventual success
Jian 蹇	303.75°	difficulty and uncertainty
Ken 艮	309.375°	halt and consideration
Qian 谦	315°	progress and success
Fou 否	320.625°	imbalance and lack of harmony
Cui 萃	326.25°	uncertainty and rejuvenation
Jin 晋	331.875°	brilliance and peace
Yu 豫	337.5°	control, discipline and success
Guan 观	343.125°	superficial great success; moderate progress
Bi 比	348.75°	good fortune and progress
Bao 剥	354.375°	halt and insecurity

Note: It is not good practice to orient a building to face true north, east, south or west. If it is auspicious to place it in the direction of *Kun*, then place it off north (between 1° and 5° off north).

The *Yi Jing* orientations should be adopted with reference to the external environment. Even though an orientation is auspicious, if there are external elements affecting it adversely, another more suitable orientation should be adopted.

Five Elements	Time of Birth	Orientation
Wood	11 pm – 1 am 1 am – 3 am	north north-northeast
Fire	3 am – 5 am 5 am – 7 am	east-northeast east
Earth	7 am – 9 am 9 am – 11 am	east-southeast south-southeast
Gold	11 am – 1 pm 1 pm – 3 pm	south south-southwest
Water	3 pm – 5 pm 5 pm – 7 pm 7 pm – 9 pm 9 pm – 11 pm	west-southwest west west-northwest north-northwest

The three most important wall openings of a building are the main gate, main door and the back door. For centuries, man has stressed the importance of the gateway and the main entrance. The Romans built triumphal arches whenever they had a victory or conquered a city. Church builders constructed elaborate portals around the entrances of churches. The Japanese built entrance gates with elaborate brackets and complicated structural beams and frames. The Indians constructed gopurams with tiers of sculptured animals, figurines and symbols to mark the entrance of a Hindu temple. The Chinese place much importance to the main entrance as they believe that it is like the mouth of a person. If *sheng qi* enters a commercial house through the door, the company would have good business, but if *si qi* (breath that indicates death and imbalance) enters it, the company would suffer from poor business.

When building or buying your business premises, examine the elements in front of the intended or existing main entrance. There is a lack of balance of *qi* at the entrance of the building if the centre of the front door faces the edge of a commercial building and empty land as shown in the diagram below.

Steep or pointed roof form or gable end causes *sha qi* to the entrance. See diagrams below for further examples of poor placing of front door.

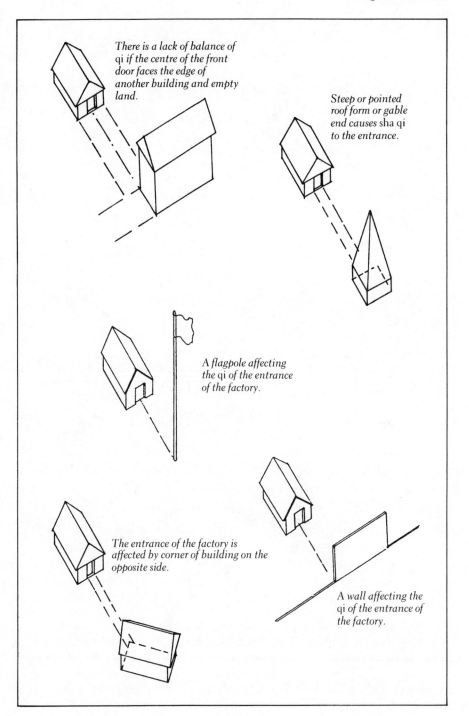

There is a lack of balance of qi if the centre of the front door faces the edge of another building and empty land.

Steep or pointed roof form or gable end causes sha qi to the entrance.

A flagpole affecting the qi of the entrance of the factory.

The entrance of the factory is affected by corner of building on the opposite side.

A wall affecting the qi of the entrance of the factory.

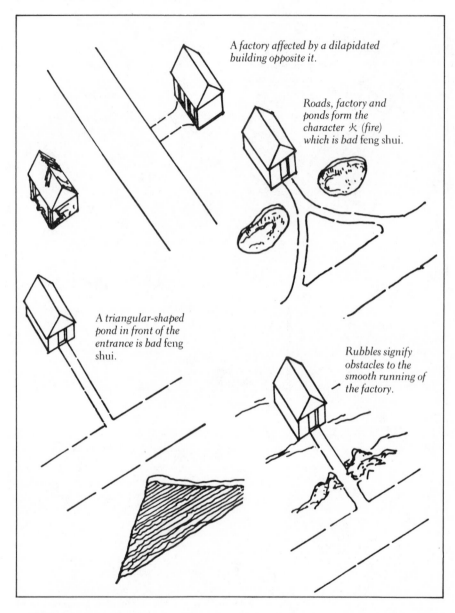

A factory affected by a dilapidated building opposite it.

Roads, factory and ponds form the character 火 (fire) which is *bad* feng shui.

A triangular-shaped pond in front of the entrance is *bad* feng shui.

Rubbles signify obstacles to the smooth running of the factory.

The Chinese have a common saying *da shu zhe yin* 大树遮阴 meaning a big tree gives shade. In *feng shui*, trees can shield a building from bad environmental influences or they can obstruct good *qi* from entering the building depending on their position in relation to the building. The following sketches illustrate the effects of trees on commercial buildings.

A *withering tree in front of the door is bad* feng shui.

An *awkwardly shaped tree in front of the door is bad* feng shui.

Both factories are protected by the trees.

4   *Feng Shui* and the Design of Buildings

Feng shui analysis for commercial projects should be done during the initial or schematic design stage so that the building design can be developed to respond to the conditions of the site — the cosmological as well as the physical environment. This reduces changes to the minimal at the detailed design development stage, saving both manpower and time and, therefore, cost.

Space and scale in commercial buildings should have a sense of balance because people who visit them rely on this sense of balance to move comfortably within them. There are two forms of balance: symmetrical and asymmetrical. Symmetrical balance can be achieved by applying an axis to dominate the spatial concept so that *yin* and *yang* design elements are balanced. Asymmetrical balance can be achieved by introducing *yin* and *yang* forms, colours and light in a dynamic and tensional layout to obtain equilibrium.

Because a commercial building has to attract customers and business, it has to have good *feng shui* and be attractive in spatial concept, form, texture and colour, both inside and outside. It is important to ensure that its scale, colour and design as a whole do not clash with *feng shui* precepts.

The commercial building must appeal to the visitor's emotional reactions. The customer must feel comfortable and relaxed. For example, a restaurant should have conducive lighting with absolutely no glare, soothing colour scheme and a temperature level which is not too hot or too cold.

A good *feng shui* design works towards a solution in which building and manmade elements are integrated with landscaping and natural elements as a total design. Space, form and proportion, lighting and colour, daylighting and ventilation as well as landscaping and furniture design are significant considerations. Planning and management are even more important to the *feng shui* of the building.

Form and Proportion

Form is the mould and mode of arrangement of the interior and exterior. Some famous designers have said that "form follows function" and "less is more". Form, whether internal or external, should be adapted to living condition and social pattern. Simplicity, economy and practicality with a sense of the aesthetic should be the principles of design. A building should be a part of the natural environment and landscape. Its form should be balanced and pleasing to the eye. It may have an open plan concept and achieve visual continuity between the inside and outside spaces.

Proportion and measurement of the human body (anthropometry) and the *feng shui* dimensional coordination should be studied and applied to interior space and furniture design since the users' and occupants' comfort is of primary importance.

A number of building forms have come to be associated with the symbolic significance of *feng shui*. It is believed that certain forms are auspicious or unlucky. Balanced and unbalanced forms have different *feng shui* connotations. For centuries balance through the positive (*yang* and solid) and the negative (*yin* and void) elements is often used by Eastern as well as Western designers to achieve equilibrium between components of built forms. The diagrams below can be described as symmetry based on an axial line.

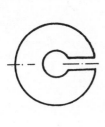 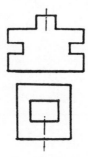 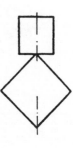

The diagrams below represent balance based on biaxial lines.

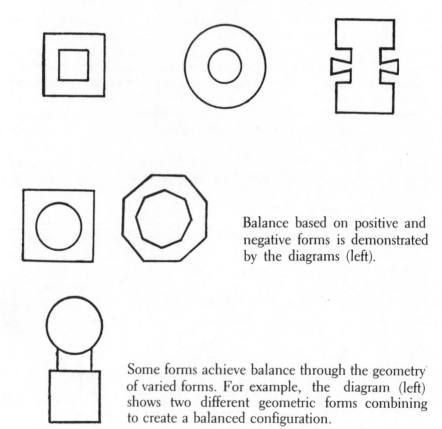

Balance based on positive and negative forms is demonstrated by the diagrams (left).

Some forms achieve balance through the geometry of varied forms. For example, the diagram (left) shows two different geometric forms combining to create a balanced configuration.

Besides balance the symbolism of the configuration must also be taken into consideration because not all balanced shapes and forms spell good luck. Some plan forms and their significance are shown below.

Diagram	Significance
	Good because it represents *kou* 口 (mouth) and symbolises posterity.
	Good because it symbolises heavenly blessing.
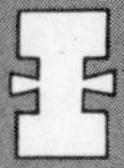	Good because it resembles the Chinese character *wang* 王 (king).
	Good because it means *ji* 吉 (luck).
	Good because the circle represents heaven and the square, earth.
	Not favourable because it resembles a butterfly which lives a short life.
	Not favourable because it resembles the character *xia* 下 (downward).

Diagram	Significance
	Not favourable because it is incomplete.
	Not favourable because it is triangular.
	Not favourable because it resembles the character *xiong* 凶 (bad luck).
	Not favourable because a cross symbolises difficulty.
	Not favourable because the portion marked x receives too vibrant *qi* (*sha qi*) from the passage y.
	Not favourable for small establishment because the shape is too powerful for a small organisation.
	Not favourable because the square is affected by the other square at a.

Lighting and Colour

Lighting and colour are particularly important in interior design and furnishing to create a place which is visually pleasing, and in which one feels comfortable and relaxed.

The feeling of space cannot be conceived without proper lighting. Therefore, the design succeeds or fails depending on the way the interior is lit. Without proper lighting, the interior appears gloomy and uninteresting. The interior space should be appropriately lit by daylight and artificial light. Light enables the perceiver to realise objects by their shapes, their finishing materials and their texture and colour. Whether comfort, relaxation and good visibility in a room are felt or not depends a great deal on how it receives its light. The room may be made hard (*yang*) or soft (*yin*), its atmosphere warm (*yang*) or cold (*yin*), exciting (*yang*) or soothing (*yin*) by appropriate lighting.

But light should not be regarded as merely a tool by the interior designer. It should be used to advantage for the psychological effect of light and colour on the users. It is light that enables man to perceive contrast, and to recognise forms and colours which determine the depth of perception of things.

One of the functions of colours is to assist good lighting and vision. Colours serve to control the level and distribution of reflected light. The interplay of light and colours should afford optimum conditions of vision for work, making it physically and mentally easier. In *feng shui*, the significance and symbolism of colours are important. Each colour has its significance. Red is auspicious, green represents longevity, yellow, authority, blue, heavenly blessings, and white, purity.

Colours are also *yin* or *yang*. *Yang* colours are red, yellow, reddish purple and yellowish-red while *yin* colours are green, blue, greenish blue, purple-blue and grey. Contrast of *yin* and *yang* colours, to achieve balance, should be made with colours of equal strength (ie the same lightness or darkness). However, when strong colours are used, the contrast created should not be so sharp as to cause discomfort or dazzle to the eyes.

The Pinetree town and country club — its membership increased after its feng shui was improved.

The Federal Reserve Bank building, Minneapolis, U.S.A. A catenary arch not only gives the building dramatic and sculptural qualities but also yin and yang expressions on the facade. (See yin/yang elements and feng shui on page 6)

The Lincoln Centre consists of three separate buildings, each featuring structural bays of related widths. The podiums on the first floor are of similar height.

Guggenheim Museum, New York. Frank Lloyd Wright, America's famous architect, designed this buildi
to express continuity of nature, homogeneity of materials and organic elegance. This egg shell-like organic
form is also favourable for feng shui *as it reduces sharp corners and edges. (See form and proportion on p4*

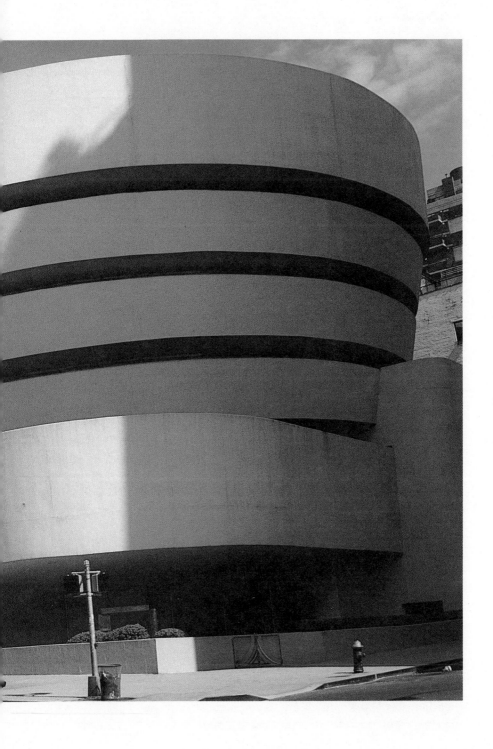

Daylighting and Ventilation

The quantity of light reaching an indoor point is related to that outside. The light inside is made up of direct light (sky illumination) and the reflected light. Daylighting is welcome into the interiors but care should be taken to reduce glare.

Glare conditions are most serious when the sky is seen against relatively dark surroundings. Discomfort is caused when sunlight falls on large reflective surfaces and raises their luminosity to very high levels. Glare should be minimised by the provision of a gradual transition from the high brightness of the sky through a window to the lower levels of brightness inside the room. Discomfort glare is reduced if the windows have deep hoods or are protected by overhangs.

Apart from the need to receive an acceptable level of lighting within the interior, the distribution of light at various distances from the window should also be considered at the design stage. The width and height of the windows should be carefully planned to achieve the required daylight factors.

An uncomfortable interior environment affect adversely the health and creativity of the occupants. Unconducive environment leads potential successful businessmen to failure because of affected health and happiness. The *qi* of the immediate and surrounding environment can affect the energy and drive of the occupants adversely or otherwise. Thus *qi* should be properly channeled from the exterior to the interior through doors, windows, vents, walls, screens and indoor plants.

Landscaping

Chinese courtyard gardens, and later Japanese gardens (as early as the Heian period 784-1185 A.D.), were designed according to *feng shui* precepts. The laws and order of nature are applied to courtyard gardens to achieve the balance between *yin* and *yang* in the layout and detailing so that the users of the gardens are in complete harmony and peace with the natural cosmological and manmade environment.

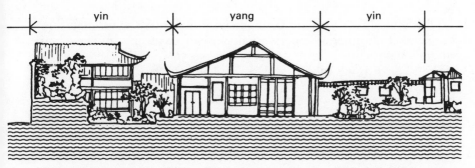

This section shows the balance of yin *(landscaped area) and* yang *(built up area) of a complex.*

Ponds, rockeries and pavilions are Chinese garden elements.

A landscaped courtyard in a commercial complex is designed mainly to complement its interior environment and to create an ambience in harmony with nature.

The main features of a landscape garden or internal courtyard may include the following:

- a pond for rearing tortoises and fish as well as for the growth of lotus to depict success and integrity
- islands in the pond to depict continuity
- rockeries to depict mountains and hills as *feng shui* elements
- streams to symbolise wealth
- plants of good symbolic significance
- trees in large courtyards to represent strength

Hills represented by rockeries have always been regarded as the source of life because they provide man with supply of water for irrigation. They are regarded as *yang* and should be complemented by *yin* features such as ponds.

The most important elements of a Chinese landscape are "hills" and "water", represented by rockeries and ponds, preferably teeming with live fish. On the pond, pavilions may be placed as focal points and to counterbalance the *yin* element, water.

Shapes assert *feng shui* influence on people and the environment, and it is good practice to shape a pond rectangular or square which resemble the character *kou* 口 meaning mouth and symbolising people and posterity. However, it is bad practice to plant a large tree on an island in a pond as the tree (*mu* 木) in the rectangular pond (*kou* 口) becomes *kun* 困 or confinement and trouble. Streams flow from north to south because north is associated with the Water Element.

Symbols of traditional Chinese values such as stork for longevity, bat for luck and tortoise for youthfulness and longevity are also used in Chinese garden design. Bronze sculptures of deer represent luck and wealth while lions, power and authority.

For the Chinese trees and plants too have symbolic significance:

Plant	Symbolism
pine	longevity
willow	grace
wutong	uprightness
plum	beauty and youth
pear	longevity
cypress	royalty
acacia	stability
ta	faithfulness
pomegranate	fertility
tangerine	wealth
camellia	evergreen
loquat	wealth
peony	wealth
bamboo	youth
orchid	endurance
peach	friendship
jasmine	friendship
rose	beauty
narcissus	rejuvenation

Some trees and plants are classified by the Chinese as either *yin* or *yang:*

Plant	*Yin/yang* Element
peony	*yang*
orchid	*yang*
peach	*yang*
willow	*yang*
chrysanthemum	*yang*
acacia	*yang*
wutong	*yang*
date	*yang*
persimmon	*yang*
cherry	*yang*
bamboo	*yang*
maple	*yang*
camphor	*yin*
banana	*yin*
grapes	*yin*
papaya	*yin*
pear	*yin*
blackwood	*yin*

Trees and plants should be planted according to *feng shui* rules. For example, willows are not to be planted in the interior courtyard and *wutong* and peach are not to be planted in front of the building.

The positioning of rockeries, trees, car parks and fish ponds should be determined with careful consideration. Geomancers have general rules of application as listed below.

A tick (√) indicates a favourable position while a cross (×) indicates an unfavourable position. A dash (−) indicates neutrality.

Position	Rockeries	Fish Ponds	Trees	Car parks
East	×	√	√ (willow)	√
Southeast	×	√	√ (bamboo)	√
South	×	√	×	×
Southwest	×	−	×	×
West	√	−	×	×
Northwest	√	√	×	√
North	√	×	−	×
Northeast	√	×	×	√

On the position of trees and its influence on *feng shui,* also refer to page 41 in the previous chapter.

Walls which enclose the compound of a building can be good or bad depending on how they are constructed in relation to the building. Wall enclosures should be proportional in height and width to the building.

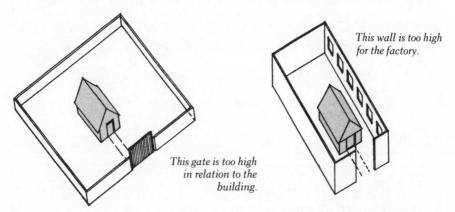

This gate is too high in relation to the building.

This wall is too high for the factory.

For example, if the building is a single storeyed factory, the enclosing wall should not be over two metres high. But if the building is 10 storeyed the wall around its compound should be over two metres in height. Also pay attention to the gate which should be proportional in size and height to the scale of the building. Wall enclosures should not be completed before the building.

A wall enclosure with open courtyards in the central space is a good feature. So are low walls built in appropriate height and without openings except for entry doors. A wall enclosure is bad *feng shui* if it surrounds the entire building with a narrow space between the wall and building. High walls with many openings along them are also bad.

Planning

In planning commercial projects the operational requirements have to be translated into spatial provisions in accordance with *feng shui* precepts. A table which indicates the favourable and unfavourable positions of staircases, parking areas, fountains, toilets and front doors is shown below. But it must be read together with the assessment of the surrounding environment and the study of the particular building or the overall layout of the cluster of buildings on the same site.

	favourable	unfavourable
front door	according to horoscope or *Yi Jing*	northeast or southwest
toilet		north, northeast, southwest or fronting the main entrance
carparks	east, southeast or northwest	north

	favourable	unfavourable
staircase		north, northwest or centre
kitchen/canteen	east, southeast, south or southwest	north

Note: the orientation is made from the centre of the building.

There are general observations that can be made for good *feng shui*.

- Entrances should be oriented according to the owner's horoscope or with reference to the *Yi Jing* (for public companies). However, the orientation should be made with reference to the surrounding environment. For example, if the orientation (according to the owner's horoscope) is to be east but the ground is hilly in that direction, then a compromise may have to be made considering the important factors regarding the site. Entrances should, whenever possible, be placed at the *qi* area and should be shielded from direct weather penetration. They are preferred not to be placed in the northeast or southwest directions.

- Windows should be protected from solar or extreme heat or cold. They should be placed to capture *qi* and encourage the flow of ventilation.

- Natural lighting should be effective and enhance space and colour. It must not be a source of glare.

- Cashier's desks are not to be placed parallel to the front entrance. They should be well lit and easily seen.

- Staircases are preferably not located in the northwesterly part or the centre of the complex. They should not directly confront entrances.

Staircases or escalators should not directly confront entrances.

- Carparking areas are not to be in the north. Kitchens too are not to be located in the north. Toilets are best not placed in the northeast.

The above are general rules of thumb. There are exceptional cases depending on other influencing factors such as noise source, view, wind direction and positioning of external elements.

Office blocks

For office blocks, the choice of the right location is of vital importance. Prime sites at the heart of the urban areas are appropriate locations. Prominent, attractive and easily accessible locations are considered good *feng shui* features. Doing the right thing involves a market survey to find out the supply and demand situation so that the right type of building is proposed, for example, mixed development or otherwise, high or low density. The type of tenants available in the market and the potential demand are important information at the design stage of the office block.

The timing is also of vital importance as the adage, the early bird catches the worm, applies to the marketing of office space. The developer should capitalise on the increase in demand for office accommodation as a result of an upturn in the economy.

The general rules of *feng shui* apply to office blocks. The main entrance lobby, access, circulation, and carparking facilities must be considered with reference to pages 58 and 59.

The floor space should be easily and efficiently subdivided to allow for easy circulation, efficient electrical and mechanical services, flexible planning and partitioning, easy access to fire escapes and lift cores. The spatial planning must be efficient and conducive for work. Amenity areas and washing facilities must be provided to serve all offices. Other services such as staff canteens, executive restaurants and refreshment areas should also be provided.

Landscaping always complements *feng shui* because it soothes the eyes and relaxes the spirit. It can be provided on a deck or on the roof or even within the office spaces.

Hotels

As far as *feng shui* is concerned the hotel should be well planned according to *feng shui* precepts of balance, harmony and appropriate orientation.

Attractive landscape elements, art ornaments and furnishings may enhance the entrances but they must be carefully chosen so as not to destroy the *feng shui* of the hotel.

The entrance should also have a sense of spaciousness and should be well lit. It should not be adversely affected by undesirable *feng shui*

elements such as sharp corners, staircases or free standing columns
pointing in its direction so that access and the flow of *qi* are not
obstructed. Its colour scheme should be balanced and symbolically
auspicious.

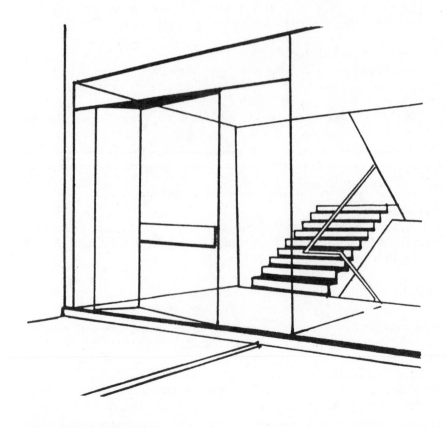

Hotel entrance reoriented to be at an angle to the staircase rather than directly facing it.

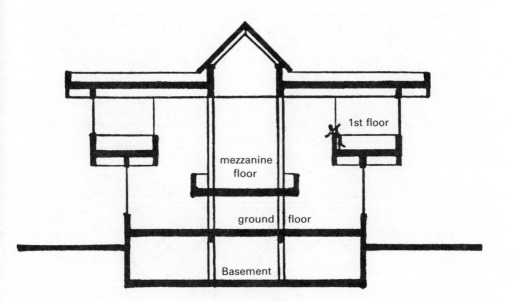

*The section of this shopping centre
resembles the character* 吉 *which augurs success.*

Shopping centres

In a shopping centre, it is important to sustain the interest of the shoppers so that they are attracted to walk right through the centre. A good layout achieves ease of circulation, provides attractive stimulus yet avoids turbulent or disturbing symbols and encourages shoppers to go through the entire shopping complex. Magnet and popular stores may be located at the ends of a mall to encourage the flow of customers from one end to another and various types of shops should be arranged on the same level. For visual communication between the floors (ie shoppers on one level can see the shops on other levels) multi-level shopping may prove successful. The following is a good example as the section resembles the word *ji* 吉 meaning successful.

If shop lots are rectangular or square ensure that the corners of the square are not exerting adverse influence on the surrounding shops as shown below.

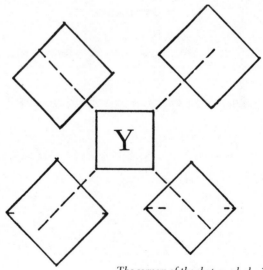

The corners of the shop marked y is
affecting the other shops around it.

Design of shops

In designing a shop, keep in mind that the ratio of circulation to display and utility space should preferably be 1 to 5.

Mirrors must be positioned with care as they are very reflective elements. A mirror that faces the entrance of the shop can create *sha qi* in the interior.

Other rules of *feng shui* also apply (refer to section on planning).

Book shop

While general rules of *feng shui* apply in the design of book shops, the special requirements are:

- Books must be well classified so that customers will not be confused.

- Display shelves must be properly and appropriately made to dimensions suggested below.

- Ventilation must be efficient so that there is plenty of fresh air in the shop and there is little moisture in the air. Dampness in unventilated spaces give rise to dry rot.

Some favourable dimensions for book display shelves

Height	Length	Breadth
108 cm	89 cm	38 cm
125 cm	108 cm	39 cm
146 cm	125 cm	40 cm
190 cm	147 cm	42 cm

Jewellery shop

Security in a jewellery shop must be well provided. Security doors and grilles in mild steel, aluminium or plate glass must be provided at strategic areas. Some favourable dimensions for security and strong room doors are 133 cm, 177 cm and 210 cm for width and 210 cm for height.

Strong rooms and safes should be located in the *qi* areas.

Hairdressing salon

- Prominent signs and advertisment are important aids to the success of a hairdressing salon.

- The reception area must be well-lit and attractive complete with facilities for storage cubicles for customers' belongings.

- Seats for the customers must be well designed to geomantic dimensions to provide comfort and ease. (See page 74 for dimensions.)

- Shampoo and washing areas should be positioned so that customers feel relaxed and do not suffer glare from the sun.

Shoe shop

- Special attention should be paid to the display of shoes which should be divided in sections (i.e. children's, men's and women's).

- Shoes should be displayed at eye level or within easy vision of the customers.

- Shoe shelves should be inclined to 5°, dimensions can follow those for book shelves (see page 65).

- Mirrors should not be placed facing the front door so as to cause *sha qi*. Foot mirrors are to be inclined at an angle of about 23° − 25°.

- Foot stools should not be placed in positions which could cause an obstruction to circulation or *qi*.

- The reception or cash counter is an important element in the shop and should be placed in the *qi* area or in a strategic position.

Industrial buildings

In designing industrial buildings it is important to ensure that the

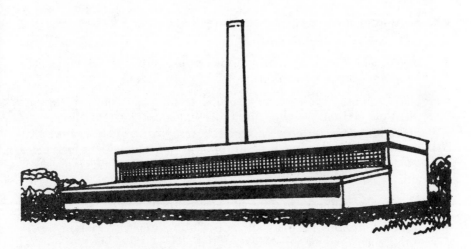

Placement of tall chimneys must be made with due consideration to feng shui.

intangible and tangible aspects of architecture achieve balance of beneficial *qi* and has no harmful influences from external forces. Balance must be obtained between the material reality of economy and the desirability of safety for workers and for the physical environment of the industrial estate. The choice of building materials and the placement of furnaces, chimneys and kilns have to be made not only on functional and aesthetic but also *feng shui* considerations.

For example, if a very reflective wall finish is used on an industrial building and this wall finish faces an office within the complex, the wall finish may cause too much *sha qi* to the office space through its windows. If the industrial complex requires the building of highrise chimneys, the placement of these chimneys must be made with due consideration to *feng shui*. They must not affect the entrances, the managers' offices, the main office or reception area and the accountant's office. They must also be of sufficient height so that pollution will not cause ill health.

Factors that may adversely influence operation efficiency are:

- poorly designed production areas (eg poorly lit, poorly ventilated and located in poor *qi* areas)

- inadequate storage or poorly located storage areas (at the end of a long corridor or T-junction)

- poor circulation (for example spatial relationship between movement of goods and loading and unloading areas. If the loading and unloading bays are poorly located or designed in such a way that those doing the loading have insufficient space to work or load the goods because those who are unloading goods are in their way, the efficiency of both are affected.)

- poor services and waste disposal and treatment

- noise pollution (sources of noise from impact, friction, air turbulence are poor *feng shui* conditions because the effects of noise pollution cause ill health).

Another important consideration is security and traffic control. The property manager must consider the safety and security of the industrial complex but in doing so he has to ensure the security features do not adversely affect the *feng shui* of the complex. When selecting an alarm system care must be taken not to install too much equipment which may easily be set off or overly sensitive otherwise the sirens going off often may cause bad *feng shui* influence in the form of noise pollution.

In the construction of an industrial complex, cost and economy are important considerations. Owing to the large spatial requirement, very often, constructional and structural systems may be confined to those which allow for speed and large spans. The following diagrams are common forms of structures for factories. *Feng shui* wise they are generally acceptable. However, for offices within the complex, there should be false ceilings so that the complicated roof structure cannot be seen within the offices.

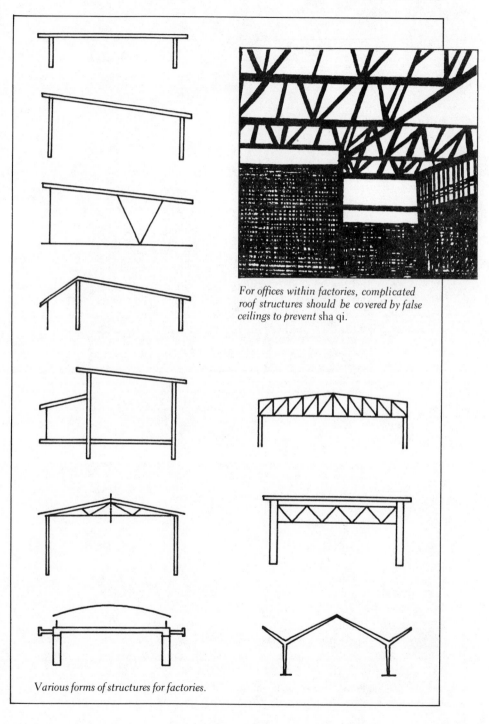

For offices within factories, complicated roof structures should be covered by false ceilings to prevent sha qi.

Various forms of structures for factories.

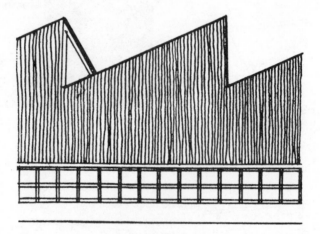

Factory with clerestory facing north.

One of the popular roof forms for factories is the asymmetrical pitched roof which allows daylight from the clerestory. Care must be taken to reduce glare from the light source and the building must be oriented so that the clerestory faces north or south.

Design of offices

The moods and emotions of office occupiers are also part of the *feng shui* of a place. Lighting, furnishing, temperature, weather and sound control that affect the ambience of the office are *feng shui* features.

Good visibility and even distribution of light are necessary for efficient performance. It is good practice to have general lighting to give an even distribution of light for the entire work space. Localised lighting may be added for special areas that require it for specific work to be done. However, there should not be glare or harsh shadows created as a result.

Mounting height of lights should be determined to give the required light level. The following measurements are auspicious:

241 cm from floor
253 cm   "   "
261 cm   "   "
275 cm   "   "
280 cm   "   "
300 cm   "   "

Furniture layout and dimensioning are also important aspects affecting the *feng shui* of the business establishment.

When designing the offices of important managers and directors, their horoscopes should be consulted to ensure that they are in harmony in their offices. The orientation of their work tables and chairs should be placed to achieve harmony and balance with the surrounding environment. The table on page 72 refers to the orientation compatible with the year of birth of the person concerned.

Besides orientation and placement of furniture, the colour scheme of the room must be compatible with the user. The following table provides some ideas on suitable colour schemes for users.

Horoscope	Colours
Rat	white, red, green
Ox or Tiger	yellow, white, red
Rabbit	white, red, purple
Dragon or Snake	white, green, red
Horse	white, green, red
Goat or Monkey	white, green, yellow
Rooster	white, red, yellow
Dog or Pig	yellow, white, red

Note: Black or dark colours are to be used in small areas.

Qi orientations for males								
SW	E	SE	SW	NW	W	NE	S	N
1917	1916	1915	1914	1913	1912	1911	1910	1909
1926	1925	1924	1923	1922	1921	1920	1919	1918
1935	1934	1933	1932	1931	1930	1929	1928	1927
1944	1943	1942	1941	1940	1939	1938	1937	1936
1953	1952	1951	1950	1949	1948	1947	1946	1945
1962	1961	1960	1959	1958	1957	1956	1955	1954
1971	1970	1969	1968	1967	1966	1965	1964	1963
1980	1979	1978	1977	1976	1975	1974	1973	1972
1989	1988	1987	1986	1985	1984	1983	1982	1981
1998	1997	1996	1995	1994	1993	1992	1991	1990
2007	2006	2005	2004	2003	2002	2001	2000	1999
2016	2015	2014	2013	2012	2011	2010	2009	2008
2025	2024	2023	2022	2021	2020	2019	2018	2017
2034	2033	2032	2031	2030	2029	2028	2027	2026
2043	2042	2041	2040	2039	2038	2037	2036	2035
2052	2051	2050	2049	2048	2047	2046	2045	2044

Year of Birth (for males table)

Qi orientations for females								
SE	E	SW	N	S	NE	W	NW	NW
1917	1916	1915	1914	1913	1912	1911	1910	1909
1926	1925	1924	1923	1922	1921	1920	1919	1918
1935	1934	1933	1932	1931	1930	1929	1928	1927
1944	1943	1942	1941	1940	1939	1938	1937	1936
1953	1952	1951	1950	1949	1948	1947	1946	1945
1962	1961	1960	1959	1958	1957	1956	1955	1954
1971	1970	1969	1968	1967	1966	1965	1964	1963
1980	1979	1978	1977	1976	1975	1974	1973	1972
1989	1988	1987	1986	1985	1984	1983	1982	1981
1998	1997	1996	1995	1994	1993	1992	1991	1990
2007	2006	2005	2004	2003	2002	2001	2000	1999
2016	2015	2014	2013	2012	2011	2010	2009	2008
2025	2024	2023	2022	2021	2020	2019	2018	2017
2034	2033	2032	2031	2030	2029	2028	2027	2026
2043	2042	2041	2040	2039	2038	2037	2036	2035
2052	2051	2050	2049	2048	2047	2046	2045	2044

Year of Birth (for females table)

Furniture

In choosing furniture for your business some practical points should be considered. Furniture should be comfortable and should fit well into the space it is meant for. As maintenance cost is an important factor, furniture should require minimum upkeep, and when meant for public spaces such as lobbies of shopping centres, should be vandal-proof.

Shapes and sizes of furniture should conform to *feng shui* rules. (See diagrams below.)

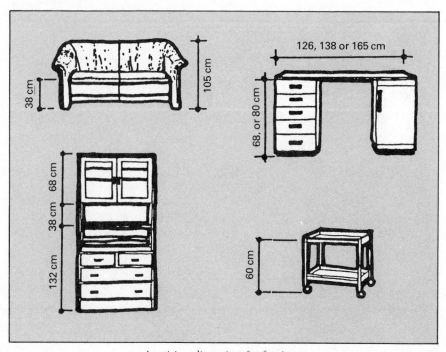

Auspicious dimensions for furniture.

Auspicious dimensions for furniture.

Management

The management of the business establishment is an important component of *feng shui*. For a business house the administerial and production and sales functions are very important to the success of the business. Therefore besides the design factors, the human factor is also to be considered if success is to be achieved.

Thus from the start the operational requirements must be met to facilitate staff efficiency and cooperation.

Efficiency may be achieved through well planned circulation and space planning. For example, how the manager's office is related to the secretariat or how the conference rooms are located with reference to the staff rooms.

Cooperation among staff members may be achieved by grouping people of compatible horoscopes to work together rather than forcing people who are incompatible to work as a team. A personnel list may be drawn so that people can be posted to the appropriate department accordingly.

5   *Feng Shui* Names and Signboards for Commercial Buildings

Names

The name of a business establishment is very important because it represents the company. If the name spells "luck" and "confidence" it gives spiritual aspiration to the management. If it spells ill omen it exerts psychological worry. It is necessary to choose an auspicious and meaningful name that has balance of *yin* and *yang*. The number of strokes in the name also should be carefully considered. For example, a six-character name should be made up of characters of *yang*, *yang*, *yin*, *yang*, *yin* and *yin* combination or *yin*, *yin*, *yang*, *yin*, *yang* and *yang*. Whether a character is *yin* or *yang* depends on the number of strokes in it. Odd numbers are *yang* and even, *yin*.

The Five Elements (gold, wood, water, fire and earth) influence the seasons and names of establishments. To arrive at the Element the sound of the character is assessed.[1] Gold characters begin with c, q, r, s, x or z (these are read not as in the English alphabet but in pinyin). Wood characters begin with g or k; water with b, f, h, m or p; fire with d, j, l, n, t or z (note: z is both gold and fire); and earth with a, w, y, e, or o. It is favourable to have water with wood, wood with fire, fire with earth, earth with gold and gold with water. It is not favourable to combine earth with water, water with fire, fire with gold, gold with wood and wood with earth.

Once the *yin/yang* elements and the Five Elements are in harmony the total number of strokes in the name may be checked. The auspicious numbers are:

> 3, 5, 6, 6, 8, 11, 13, 15, 16, 17, 18, 21, 23, 24, 25, 29, 31,
>
> 32, 33, 35, 37, 39, 48, 52, 63, 65, 67, 68, 73, 75, 77, 78, 80,
>
> 81, 83, 84, 87, 88, 89, 90, 91, 92, 97, 98, 99, 100.

Some examples of name analysis are given below.

Example 1.

Da	Zong	Si	Ping	Gong	Yue
大	衆	食	品	工	業
3	12	9	9	4	13
yang	*yin*	*yang*	*yang*	*yin*	*yang*

You	Xian	Gong	Si
有	限	公	司
6	9	4	5
yin	*yang*	*yin*	*yang*

Meaning of name: Everyone's Food Industry Ltd Company.

Analysis:
The total number of strokes in the name amounts to 73 and the Elements are fire, fire, gold, water, wood, earth, earth, gold, wood, gold.

Although there is more *yang* than *yin* in the name it can be considered as fairly well balanced. The total number of strokes in the name, 73, spells luck. The Element fire is followed by the Element gold which is not very compatible with it. The fifth character wood and sixth, earth, are also incompatible. Thus this name is not very auspicious.

Example 2:

You	Wang	Gu	Fen	You	Xian	Gong	Si
有	望	股	份	有	限	公	司
6	11	8	6	6	9	4	5
yin	*yang*	*yin*	*yin*	*yin*	*yang*	*yin*	*yang*

Meaning of name: Hopeful Securities Ltd Company.

Analysis:
The total number of strokes in the name is 55 which is not a very lucky number. In this name there is more *yin* than *yang* but it can still be considered as fairly balanced. The Elements in this name are earth, earth, wood, water, earth, gold, wood, gold. The sixth and seventh characters, *xian gong*, are in conflict. The rest of the characters are neutral. Therefore this name is considered as average in terms of *feng shui*.

Example 3:

Fa	Li	Shi	Wu	Suo
友	利	事	務	所
5	7	8	10	8
yang	*yang*	*yin*	*yin*	*yin*

Meaning of name: Prosperity and Success Agency

Analysis:
The total number of strokes in the name is 38 and the Elements are water, fire, gold, earth and gold. In this name the first two characters clash. Perhaps if the first character is changed to *yi* 熠 (15 strokes, *yang* and earth) the name is even better and more balanced.

No wonder this company has closed down. Look at the name — it's Kuai Dou — 'Collapse Quickly'!

Signboards

The signboard is a very important element for a business establishment because it represents the spirit and nature of business of the company. It must be legible and well-balanced in size, proportion and graphic elements.

The sizes of signboards are subject to *yin* and *yang* forces. For example, if the length is *yin*, say 88 cm (even in number), then the breadth should be *yang*, say 81 cm (odd number). Below is a list showing some lucky *yin* and *yang* dimensions.

Yin 阴	**Yang** 阳
18 cm	19 cm
20 cm	21 cm
22 cm	23 cm
38 cm	39 cm
40 cm	41 cm
42 cm	47 cm
48 cm	61 cm
62 cm	67 cm
86 cm	69 cm
88 cm	81 cm
100 cm	89 cm
108 cm	125 cm
128 cm	145 cm
146 cm	147 cm

Signboards should have either three or five colours. Three symbolises growth and five, completeness. Those with two or four colours are not as ideal.

The choice of colours should be related to the orientation of the signboard as shown in the following table.

Favourable Colour of Signboard	Position of Signboard	
	favourable	unfavourable
white red green	southeast northwest	east south west north northeast
white green yellow	south	east southeast southwest west northsouth north northeast
white red purple	southeast south	east north southwest west northeast
white green red	southeast north	east southwest west northwest northeast
red yellow purple	south northwest northeast	east southeast southwest north
yellow white	southwest west	east southeast

Favourable Colour of Signboard	Position of Signboard	
	favourable	unfavourable
red	northwest northeast	
white red yellow	southwest west northwest	east southeast south northeast
yellow white red	south northsouth	east southeast north
white green red	east south southwest northeast	west northwest north

General rules on signboard designs are as follows. Signboards should:

- be pleasant and pleasing to the eye
- be balanced in shape
- not block any window or opening
- not be triangular in shape
- not be made of soft wood
- be proportional in size to the size of the building
- be securely fixed and anchored.

Orientations of signboards and their implications are summarised in the table below.

Orientations	Implications
east	Signboards in this direction are preferred to be high as the east denotes the rising of the sun.
southeast	The height of the signboard is to be moderate. If it is too high it will block the flow of *qi*.
south	Signboards to be moderately high. If they are too high they will be too *yang* and cause imbalance.
southwest	Signboards are not to be too high (6 metres above ground level is a good height).
west	Signboards to be of moderate height. If they are too low, friction among staff members within the company will result.
northwest	Signboards are to be fairly high but should not cause imbalance.
north	Signboards are to be fairly high to ensure harmony.
northeast	Signboards are to be at a low level to avoid disharmony.

The balance of the Five Elements is just as important as the *yin* and *yang*. The best combinations of the Five Elements of a three-character name are shown below:

water, wood, fire
fire, wood, water
wood, water, gold
gold, water, wood
water, gold, earth
fire, earth, gold
earth, fire, wood
wood, fire, earth
earth, gold, water
gold, earth, fire

Logos

A logo or signage on a commercial building carries a denotative indication and gives a message regarding its trade and sometimes, products.

Symbols, signs and neon lights are some of the factors that have turned Las Vegas from a desert town into a busy successful commercial centre with casino complexes, hotels, and restaurants which are humming with life.

Good signage is not only an integral part of the building design but also important in *feng shui* terms. Besides the colour and size of the signboards, the logos on them are just as important. Logos have to be identifiable, attractive and appropriate.

These two symbols could be more balanced if the black areas could be more balanced (for example, one of the black fish could be white).

This oval logo symbolises conflict. The one on the right is better as the upward arrow is balanced by the downward arrow.

A symbol that looks like an upright arrow is a lucky logo while one that looks like a downward arrow is unlucky.

The logo is not good because the central part is like a cross (to the Chinese the cross signifies problems unsolved).

A dragon symbolises power, authority and vitality.

Footnote

1 See Lip, Evelyn, *Choosing Auspicious Chinese Names*, Times Books International, Singapore, 1988.

6   Office Warming Rituals

Symbols and rituals are essential external signs to bring luck to the occupants of a new office or business establishment. The Chinese employ geomancers to select a good day and time to move into the new premises. Office warming rituals ensure that all evil spirits leave the new premises and good *qi* is brought in.

First of all an auspicious day and time is chosen for the ceremony. It should be a day in which the constellations are in such positions that they may charge the business premises with good *qi* and power. Consult the *Tong Shu* for choice of date.

On the chosen day, all windows, ventilation openings, grilles, openings in walls and skylights have to be covered with black paper or cloth so that the business house or office is in total darkness for an hour before the office warming ceremony. All animals such as dogs (except fish) are to be brought outside the premises. All electrical fittings and power points are to be switched off. Office staff should leave the premises half an hour before the chosen time. A red banner is hung over the front door across the signboard.

As the time approaches, the manager or owner starts a fire in a charcoal stove and fans it until the charcoal is red hot to symbolise the start of a booming business. At the exact moment chosen by the geomancer or stated in the *Tong Shu* he places the stove at the centre of the main doorway and walks over it with his left foot, followed by his right. His employees then follow him, walking over the stove. He then opens the door and takes down the red banner. Sometimes guests and friends are invited to be present during the ritual.

The black paper covering the openings of the office is quickly peeled off to welcome beneficial light at the chosen auspicious time. Electricity is switched on so that artificial lighting also comes on. Music can also be played. During the hour of the office warming ritual, as a symbol of office unity, employees should not leave the premises.

The opening ceremony of the Pegasus, a stained glass producer's showroom, was in accordance with a geomancer's advice.

On the day chosen by a geomancer, at the exact time of 12.07 pm, the

Office with windows and air vents sealed before office warming ritual.

A charcoal stove is placed at the centre of the main doorway for the manager or owner and his staff to walk over.

owner opened the locks of the front door, opened a bottle of champagne and switched on the lights within a short period of 45 seconds to augur good fortune.

A red banner is hung over the front door across the signboard.

The *Tong Shu* 通书

The *Tong Shu* or Chinese almanac is published every year in Hong Kong and exported to the Southeast Asian region. It gives information on many aspects of Chinese beliefs such as the writing of charms, the interpretation of dreams, the diagrammatic explanations of pregnancy and growth of a foetus, diagrammatic representations of the constellations, palmistry, fortune telling, face reading, design of greeting cards, practice for business, advice for character building, calendar for a period of one hundred years and the current calendar.

In the current calendar, both the lunar and Gregorian dates are given. Each day is divided into 12 periods, each of two hours' duration. Each period is classified as good, fairly good or bad. The day is further analysed for its suitability for purchase of property, burial of the dead, performance of ceremonies such as marriage or engagement, business opening or office warming, repair of houses or properties, paying homage to ancestors and others.

Tong Shu or Chinese almanac

7   Case Studies

Many practising architects in Southeast Asia have encountered clients who insist on altering building plans for better *feng shui*. Sometimes construction comes to a standstill so that the main door or main ridge beam of the roof can be installed at the right moment according to *feng shui*.

I encountered geomancers on many occasions as a practising architect during the 1960s. In 1966, I was the architect of a large house. My client brought in a *feng shui* master who changed the position of the staircase that originally faced the entrance hall. The front door was also realigned to suit the owner's horoscope.

The following case studies illustrate how geomancers improve the *feng shui* of buildings.

Case 1

The front door of an interior designer's office was realigned for *feng shui* purpose. It appears that business became better after adjustment of the front door was made in accordance with his horoscope.

Case 2

A consultancy firm which repairs, sells and offers consultancy in high technology aviation products is said to have experienced a few obstacles in business. A geomancer was called in who detected external elements which were adversely affecting the *feng shui* of the company (see block layout of the company compound below).

The corner of the block marked 'x' pointed at the main entrance of the company. The layout of the office block is such that the manager cannot communicate easily with his marketing staff. So a scheme was proposed to overcome the ill effects by the reorganisation of the usage of space and repositioning of the main entrance.

The front door of an interior designer's office is realigned in accordance with his horoscope.

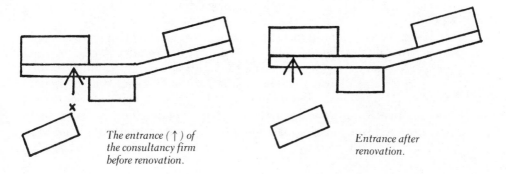

The entrance (↑) of the consultancy firm before renovation.

Entrance after renovation.

Case 3

Sometimes a business house may be well-designed with no *feng shui* defects. Yet the business is poor and the company runs into debts. In such a case, the *feng shui* of the company director's or manager's residence has to be assessed.

In just such a case, a company director's house was found to be geomantically unfavourable though built on a long axis facing north-south, a favourite orientation for houses among the Chinese.

It was found that the main door to the house was in an awkward position under a staircase. The orientation of the door was also not compatible with the owner's horoscope.

The living room, though not too small, could have been wider and more generous in spatial terms. The kitchen stove was facing the wrong direction geomantically and there was no direct access from the kitchen to the external yard for utility purpose.

On the upper level, one of the three bedrooms was situated far from the toilet. The partition between the bedrooms and the verandah was solid, depriving the rooms of cross ventilation. The roof over the entrance porch just outside the main door was not utilised.

These physical environmental factors are contrary to good *feng shui* practice. To improve the *feng shui*, a few alterations were made.

The front door was repositioned and a garden wall added to accentuate the front door.

The stove was repositioned to face east. The living room was widened by pushing the south wall out to incorporate the entrance porch into the living room. A terrace was added on the north side to further enhance the living space and allow efficient ventilation across the space. On the upper floor, solid partitions were demolished, the rooms extended and doors repositioned to allow ventilation across the rooms. The roof over the entrance porch below was made use of as a family room and a toilet was added to the third room.

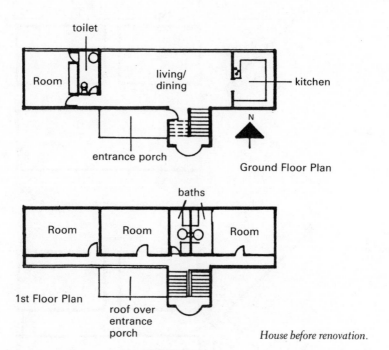

toilet

Room

living/dining

kitchen

N

Ground Floor Plan

entrance porch

baths

Room

Room

Room

1st Floor Plan

roof over entrance porch

House before renovation.

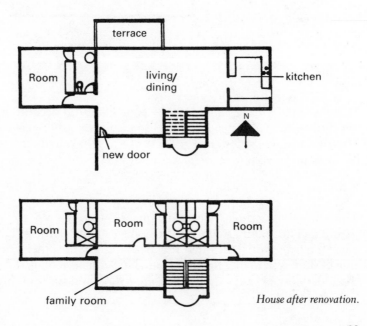

terrace

Room

living/dining

kitchen

N

new door

Room

Room

Room

family room

House after renovation.

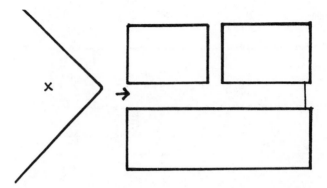

Entrance of shopping arcade before alteration.

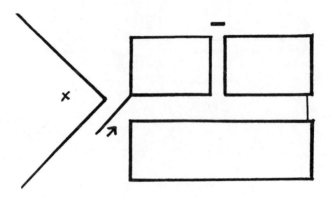

Entrance of shopping arcade after alteration.

Case 4

This shopping arcade suffered from poor *feng shui* because its entrance was disturbed by the neighbouring shop marked x (see diagram above.) The entrance was redesigned and a wall was added to direct shoppers in. Business improved.

Case 5

This shopping complex (see diagram below) is shaped in an awkward manner. The internal core of shops have many corners that adversely affect the *feng shui* of the outer ring of shops. On the other hand the outer ring of shops encircling the inner core block the flow of *qi*. The corners of the inner core of shops should be rounded off and sky vents built to bring in *qi* from above.

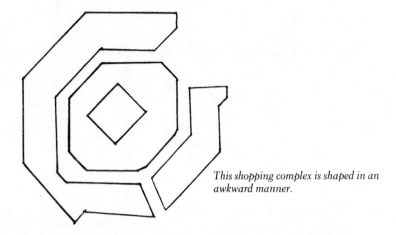

This shopping complex is shaped in an awkward manner.

Case 6

This shopping centre has too many entrances and its *feng shui* is too disperse. To improve it, one main entrance should be created with the greatest stimulus and the other entrances rendered less significant. This would also encourage shoppers to walk through as many shops as possible.

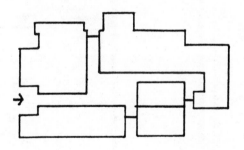

This shopping centre has too many entrances.

Case 7

Whenever sculptures are displayed in front of or inside a building, ennsure that they are shaped or placed in such a way that they do not assert bad *feng shui* or *sha qi* on the building or the interior of the building.

One such case was found where the director's and manager's offices

95

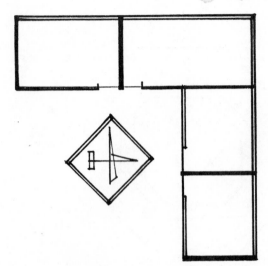

were affected by a huge sculpture placed outside the building in a square court at an oblique angle. The corners of the square court and the knife-like sculpture were pointing at the director's and manager's offices. After renovations were made and the sculpture taken out, business improved.

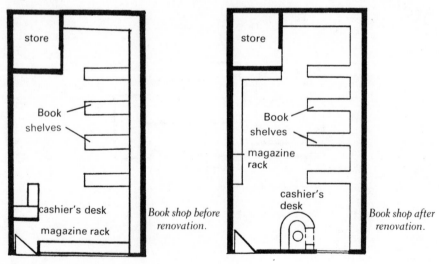

Book shop before renovation.

Book shop after renovation.

Case 8

The entrance of a book shop was affected by a magazine rack. The *qi* was oppressed by the ceiling high partitions of the cashier's desk and the magazine rack. The *feng shui* was improved by repositioning the magazine rack and cashier's desk.

Case 9

The entrance of a boutique and shoe shop is confronted by an internal staircase which causes imbalanced *qi*. The cashier below the staircase suffers from oppressive *qi*.

The *feng shui* can be improved by relocating the entrance and the cashier's counter as shown below.

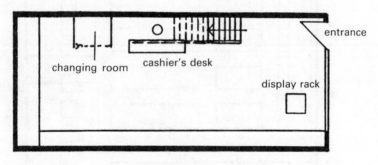

Boutique before renovation.

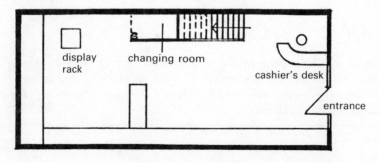

Boutique after renovation.

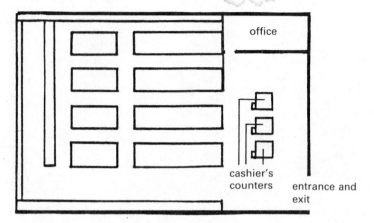

Supermarket before renovation.

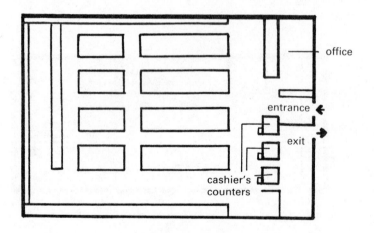

Supermarket after renovation.

Case 10

The business of a supermarket was affected by poor *feng shui*. Shoplifting occurred frequently. A reorganisation of the usage of space and repositioning of the office and cashier's counters was made. *Feng shui* and business improved.

Case 11

The management of a night club had problems with a high turnover of

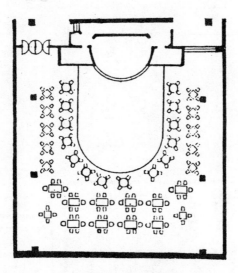

Night club before renovation.

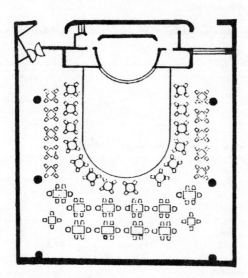

Night club after renovation.

staff and other problems. An assessment of the *feng shui* showed that *qi* was disturbed and blocked at the entrance by a large reinforced concrete column. The entrance doors were oriented true north which was in conflict with the horoscope of the owner.

After the front doors were repositioned at an auspicious angle obliquely toward northwest, the problems were resolved.

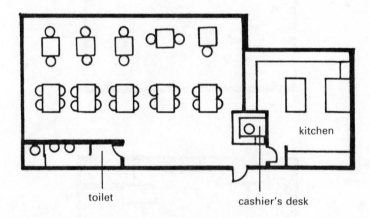

Coffee house before renovation.

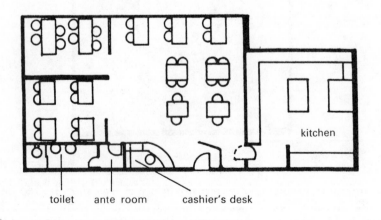

Coffee house after renovation.

Case 12

The business of a coffee house was poor. The geomancer assessed the plan of the premises as geomantically unfavourable. The door of the toilet faces the entrance space and customers entering the coffee house are confronted by the odour emanating from the toilet whenever the toilet door is opened. There is cross circulation between the waiters from the kitchen and the customers coming into the coffee house. The layout of the tables is also uneconomically planned.

The entrance and layout are redesigned for better *feng shui* and efficiency. The entrance and the cashier's desk are repositioned so that they no longer confront each other. The new entrance also eliminates the problem of cross circulation. An ante room is created where the toilet door is. The layout of the tables is improved so that more tables can be accommodated.

Case 13

The Pinetree town and country club has its membership increased substantially after its *feng shui* has been improved.

One of the improvements made was to the main entrance. A screen was built in the entrance lobby to cut off the view of some undesirable external elements and to achieve balance of *qi*. This screen also helps to harmonise the *qi* of the twin staircases.

Glossary

azure dragon	A mythical guardian of a Chinese temple always placed on the left of the building.
Five Elements	Conceived as the five forces of nature by the Chinese as early as the 4th century B.C. and designed in the sequence gold, wood, water, fire and earth, and may be positioned in the order of destruction or harmony.
qi	Cosmic breath of life for growth and vitality which causes mountains to be formed and gives man spiritual energy.
sha qi	Literally translated, breath that hurts; travels in a straight line; eg when a building faces a T-junction, the *qi* is too vibrant and becomes *sha qi*.
sheng qi	Breath that gives life and promotes growth.
si qi	Breath that indicates death and imbalance.
Tong Shu	An almanac of the days of the year, dating back to 2200 B.C., giving information on seasonal festivals, the right time to perform ceremonies such as weddings, ancestor worship; also includes information on astrology, Chinese customs, weather prediction, etc.
Yi Jing	*Book of Changes*, the first of Confucius' canons, was first edited by Emperor Fu Xi; a classic book of divination giving insight into the cosmic changes that influence man; based on the permutations of *yin* and *yang*; representations expressed in 64 hexagrams.
yin¹/yang elements	According to Chinese beliefs *yin* and *yang* elements are complementary forces that underpin all things in existence; everything in the universe can be classified as either *yin* or *yang*; masculinity, light, positiveness, are *yang* while feminity, darkness, negativeness are *yin*; when there is balance of *yin* and yang there is equilibrium and growth.

Bibliography

Chinese

Feng Shui Guai Tan 风水怪谈 , 1963
Gu Jin Tu Shu Zhi Cheng 古今图书集成 , China 中国 , 1726.
Hsiao Zhi 肃吉 , *Wu Xing Da Yi* 五行大义 , China 中国 , 600 A.D.
Huang Chao Chuan 黄朝全 , *Kanyu Ao Mi* 堪舆奥秘 , Taiwan 台弯 , 1980..
Jiang Ping Jie 蒋平楷 , *Di Li Zheng Shu* 地理正疏 , Taiwan 台弯 , 1980.
Luo Jin Xiang Jie 罗经详解 , Taiwan 台湾 , n.d.
Nan Hai Guan 南海关 , *Kanyu Xue Yuan Li* 堪舆学原理 , Hong Kong 香港 , 1971.
Qing Jia Qing 清家清 , *Jia Zai Feng Shui* 家宅风水 , n.d.
Shui Long Jing 水龙经 , n.d.
Tian Gong Kai Wu 天工开物 , China 中国, 1637 A.D.
Wang Qi Yan 王启燊 , *Di Lin Ren Jie* 地灵人杰 , Taipei 台北 , 1978.
Xie Yi Xian 谢易显 , *Yi Shu Xian Yi* 易术显义 , Hong Kong 香港 , 1978.
Xie Yi Xian, *Shu Shu Zhi Ke Xue* 术娄之科学 , Hong Kong 香港 , 1978.
Zeng Zi Nan 曾子南 , *San Yuan Di Li Tu Wen Qian Jie* 三元地理图文浅解 , Taipei 台北 , 1965.

English

Ball, Dyer, *Things Chinese*, London, 1904.
Bring, Mitchell, and Wayembergh, Josse, *Japanese Garden Design and Meaning*, McGraw Hill, New York, 1981.
De Barry, Chun and W.T., *Sources of Chinese Tradition*, London, 1960.
De Groot, *The Religious System of China*, Leyden, 1892.
Dore, Henry, *Research into Chinese Superstitions*, Vol. 4, Shanghai, 1928.
Eitel, E., *Feng Shui; or the Rudiments of Natural Science in China*, Hong Kong, 1873.
Feuchtwang, Stephen, "An Anthropological Analysis of Chinese Geomancy", Southern Materials Centre, Incorp., Taipei, 1974.
Forlag, G., *Chinese Buddhist Monasteries*, London, 1937.

Graham, David, *Folk Religion in S.W. China*, Washington, 1961.
Lip, Evelyn, *Chinese Geomancy*, Times Books International, Singapore, 1979.
Lip, Evelyn, "Geomancy and Building", *Development and Construction*, Singapore, 1977.
Lip, Evelyn, "Feng Shui, Chinese Colours and Symbolism", *Singapore Institute of Architects Journal*, Singapore, July, 1978.
Lip, Evelyn, *Chinese Temples and Deities*, Times Books International, Singapore, 1981.
Lip, Evelyn, *Chinese Temple Architecture in Singapore*, Singapore University Press, Singapore, 1983.
Lip, Evelyn, *Chinese Beliefs and Superstitions*, Graham Brash, Singapore, 1985.
Lip, Evelyn, *Feng Shui for the Home*, Times Books International, Singapore, 1985.
Lip, Evelyn, *Choosing Auspicious Chinese Names*, Times Books International, 1988.
Lip, Evelyn, *Things Chinese*, Graham Brash, 1988.
Needham, Joseph, *Science and Civilization in China*, London, 1982.
Palmer, Martin, *Tung Shu*, Century Hitchinson Ltd, London, 1986.
Skinner, Stephen, *The Living Earth Manual of Feng Shui*, London, 1982.
Van Over, Raymond, *I-Ching*, Chicago, 11971.
Wilhem, Richard, *I-Ching*, Routledge and Kegan Paul Ltd, London, 1951.
Willets, William, *Chinese Art*, London, 1958.

Index